CORMAN/POE

Interviews and Essays Exploring the Making of Roger Corman's Edgar Allan Poe films, 1960-1964

by Chris Alexander

HEADPRESS

CORMAN/POE

FOREWORD
BY ROGER CORMAN

When I revisit the Poe pictures, as I do from time to time, it's almost impossible for me to watch them without reflecting on how we made them and the friends and artists I worked so closely with. But I recognize the influence they've had and continue to have over people. Case in point: the book you're reading, which I think is a very thoughtful and insightful analysis of those films, and which was written over 60 years since the making of the first entry in the Poe series, THE FALL OF THE HOUSE OF USHER.

Am I surprised that these films continue to be discussed? In some ways I suppose I am. Several of the pictures have dated somewhat over time, I would say. But on the other hand, because we set the films in the past, a time that is unaffected by modern trends, the films remain in the past and specifically, in a fantastical version of the past we created. They have a look and feel that is unique to them.

For example, recently my wife Julie and I attended Francis Ford Coppola's birthday party. He had his entire family there, including all the children and grandchildren. Now, Francis often will screen films for the children at these gatherings, and it almost always happens that the little children will usually walk away from whatever movie is playing, after a time. But this year, he played THE RAVEN and none of them walked away at all! He was very surprised by this. Maybe what held their interest was the fact that the film is — more than any of the other Poe pictures — played for comedy. But maybe there were other reasons it fascinated them.

Either way, it was pleasing evidence that the pictures continue to endure and attract new audiences. In this book you will read much about the subtext of these films and I continue to be pleased that people are not only enjoying the films but recognizing the subtext we placed within them, something the European critics, primarily, were doing right from the start. Of course, not everyone has recognized that subtext. And to be honest, sometimes I believe perhaps people read too much subtext into the films! However, the unconscious mind works in mysterious ways and whatever unintentional deeper meanings scholars of these pictures might find might in fact be correct, a reading of what I unconsciously put in them at the time.

FOREWORD

Corman directing Elizabeth Shepherd and Vincent Price in THE TOMB OF LIGEIA.

The Poe pictures are most certainly horror films, first and foremost, with THE MASQUE OF THE RED DEATH being perhaps the most horrific (and maybe the best of them) and I am content with the pictures being called such. But there is more to them than just the horror, and we can credit the themes of Poe's original stories for much of that.

I certainly cite these pictures as highlights of my directorial career and when I think of them, I recall something Fellini once said to me. When I was distributing Fellini's AMARCORD through my New World Pictures company, he said to me, "Roger, forget distributing. You're doing a great job as a distributor, but it's just not you. You're a director…go back to directing."

I have few regrets regarding my career and the path it has taken, but when I do sto stop and reflect on the Poe pictures, and on my work as a director, part of me thinks Fellini may have been correct!

— ROGER CORMAN, MAY 2022

Corman and Price relaxing on the set of THE PIT AND THE PENDULUM.

CONTENTS

2: FOREWORD BY ROGER CORMAN

6: INTRODUCTION

10: THE FALL OF THE HOUSE OF USHER

24: THE PIT AND THE PENDULUM

40: THE PREMATURE BURIAL

52: TALES OF TERROR

68: THE RAVEN

82: THE HAUNTED PALACE

96: THE MASQUE OF THE RED DEATH

110: THE TOMB OF LIGEIA

APPENDIX

126: THE CENSORING OF THE MASQUE OF THE RED DEATH

132: POSTER GALLERY

148: INDEX

INTRODUCTION

When I was but a young child (as opposed to the considerably older child that I currently am) and just beginning my journey into my swelling horror cinema obsession, my late father told me he had seen a movie on TV in the early '70s called THE RAVEN, starring Vincent Price and Boris Karloff. He told me that he had watched it late at night, when I was a new baby, after a period in the wee small hours where I was up and crying, as babies are prone to do. Eventually, after I had gone back to sleep, and after my mother had fallen asleep as well, he took advantage of this peaceful window, popped some corn and flipped on the set to lose himself in some form of glowing distraction.

And there it was.

THE RAVEN.

He loved it and told me that he had found it so eerie and strange that the next day, he had wondered if he had dreamed seeing it, an experience no doubt accentuated by his own hazy-minded parental exhaustion. He said it was the work of a director named Roger Corman, to which my mom excitedly piped in that, as a teen in the early '60s, she and her friends would go and see Corman and American International Pictures movies at Toronto's Kingsway Theatre and then scare themselves silly taking the shortcut home through the cemetery.

I loved these stories because, outside of learning new information about a key architect of the genre, it is one of the fonder memories I have where my parents — eternally at odds and at each other's throats — were actually on the same page, collaborating on an evocative tale of cinematic experience with humor and affection. I loved that both mom and dad's proxy encounters with this Corman fella happened after dark, in those spaces and places that were divorced from the harsh lights and angles and mundane rituals of the day.

And thus, a seed was planted. My quest to watch any and eventually all Roger Corman films had begun. Of course, my interest in self-educating was hampered by the fact that the internet didn't exist, home video didn't even exist (or maybe it did, but it was early enough in the game that we didn't have our own VCR in the home) and library books on horror

INTRODUCTION

Corman directing Price and John Westbrook in THE TOMB OF LIGEIA.

and dark fantasy film history weren't necessarily common finds at my local library. Back then, in order to fully immerse yourself in any sort of strange cinema education, you had to do what I did and lay claim to the TV guide every week, scan it and highlight the pictures that were labelled "horror" or "science fiction" or "thriller" or "fantasy". I'd literally sleep with a small, AA-battery powered alarm clock and secretly wake up at the designated times to sneak downstairs and sit alone on the sofa at all hours and absorb as much as I could, often scaring myself near to death in the process, with every creak and squeak coming from other rooms alerting me to potential parental discovery, leading me to shut off the television and sit in the dark until the danger passed and I could turn it back on (usually just in time to see something memorably shocking or horrific occur). Eventually the VHS rental market became a thing, and I could start bringing home movies to watch, but the sort of weirder stuff I hungered for just wasn't readily available, at least not where I was.

One night, when I was about 11, I saw a listing (as I recall it was around the Halloween season, if not Halloween night itself) for a double dose of Corman chillers running on Buffalo's WGRZ, an after-hours program called "The Cat's Pyjamas".

I was ready.

By this time, I had Leonard Maltin's paperback movie guide attached to my body at all times and had gone down the rabbit hole memorizing titles, alternate titles, directors, casts, running times and star ratings. And I had certainly made myself aware of everything Corman had made. But I had only seen select early stuff like THE WASP WOMAN, BEAST FROM HAUNTED CAVE and LITTLE

CORMAN/POE

Joyce Jameson, Peter Lorre, Price and a cluster of co-stars behind the scenes of TALES OF TERROR.

INTRODUCTION

SHOP OF HORRORS, as they tended to show up frequently on local station weekend matinees. I adored these jazzy, creepy, compact little chillers but was DYING to see the movies that made up Corman's "Poe Cycle", among them, naturally, my white whale, THE RAVEN. Well, on that fateful night, the pair of Corman movies that were to run concurrently after the 11pm news were TALES OF TERROR and MASQUE OF THE RED DEATH, the latter a MUST SEE because Maltin's book gave it 3.5 stars and claimed it was "Bergman-esque", which sounded important, even though I had never seen a single Ingmar Bergman film (though again, I was very aware of who he was). I stayed up all night that night, pushing myself past the point of reason as I battled my body clock to make it to the end, when the first rays of sun set the sky alight. TALES was like entering another world and, to my surprise, it was not only stylish, scary and atmospheric but genuinely FUNNY too. However, it was MASQUE that did me in. A grandiose, doom-soaked drama laced with perversion and cruelty and eccentricities that terrified me, even though there was nothing overtly sensational or exploitative in it.

That night, after hours, all alone, defying TV curfews and flitting in and out of consciousness, I became not just a serious fan of Roger Corman, but a disciple for life. Later, I absorbed THE PIT AND THE PENDULUM, THE HAUNTED PALACE, THE PREMATURE BURIAL and THE TOMB OF LIGEIA. And of course, THE RAVEN, a film that connects me so profoundly to the warm memories of my father's voice and touch and warmth.

I have been lucky to be able to turn my passion for horror cinema into a life sustaining career and, through those professional adventures, managed to both interview Roger Corman at length and count both he and his brilliant partner and wife Julie, as friends. I still shake in awe when I watch his movies. I still get excited when I see his name on screen. This book you are holding is personal. It's a distilled collection of conversations I have had with Roger over the past 20 years, centered around the making of those mythical eight motion pictures we commonly refer to as the "Poe Cycle", culminating in a series of recent conversations conducted when Roger and I (and most of the planet) were confined to respective lockdowns. This book is more than a book to me. It's about the majesty of those remarkable movies themselves, it's about the history and impact of what Roger and his evolving tribe of creators accomplished and it's about putting our shared words and my thoughts together in one comprehensive printed document.

But more than that, it's about that time, when I was eight years old and the two people I cared about most in the world were together and laughing and sharing stories of discovering Roger, after dark.

Thank you, Roger, for that.

Thanks for all of it.

This book is for you.

– CHRIS ALEXANDER

THE FALL OF THE HOUSE OF USHER

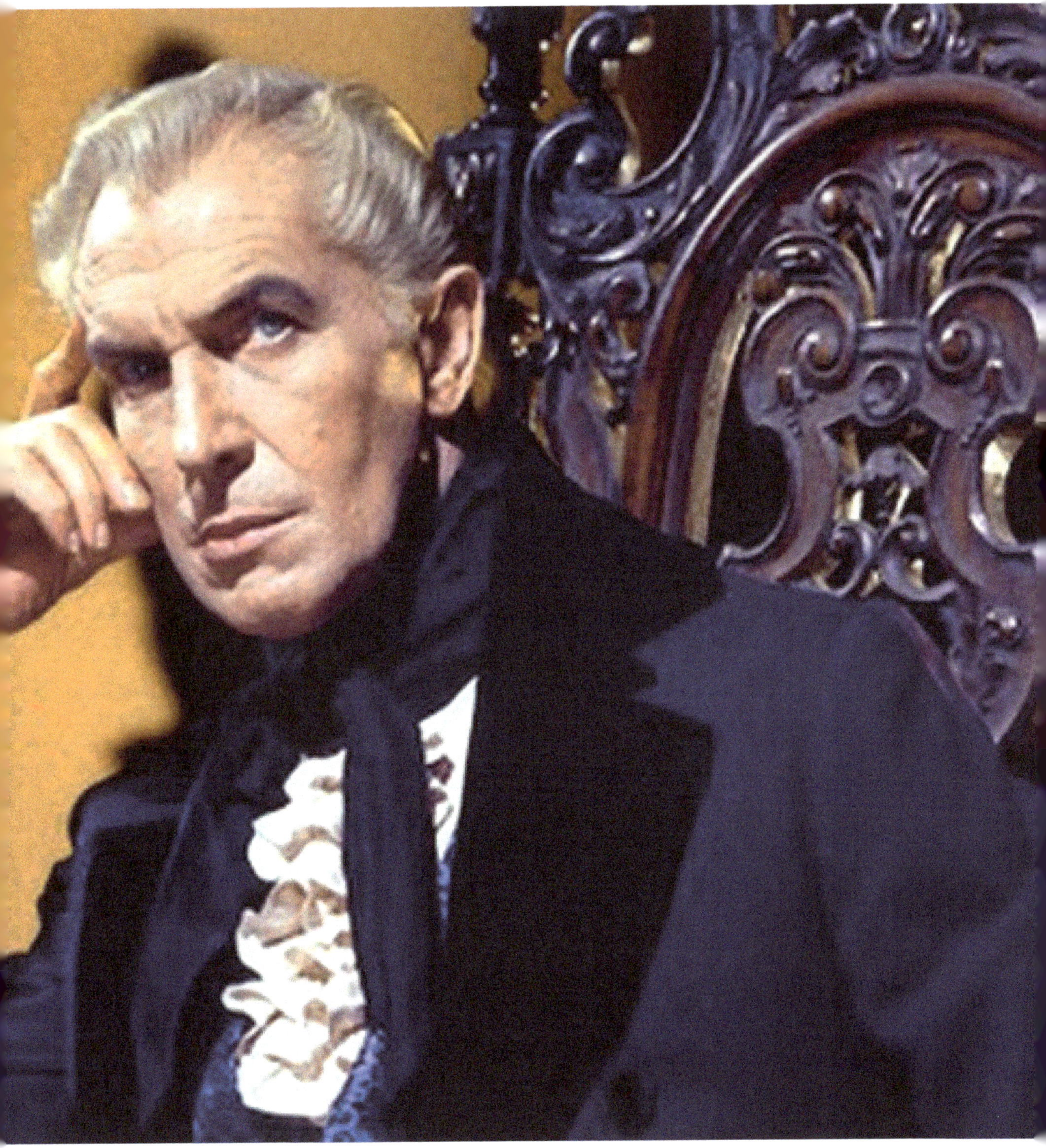

CORMAN/POE

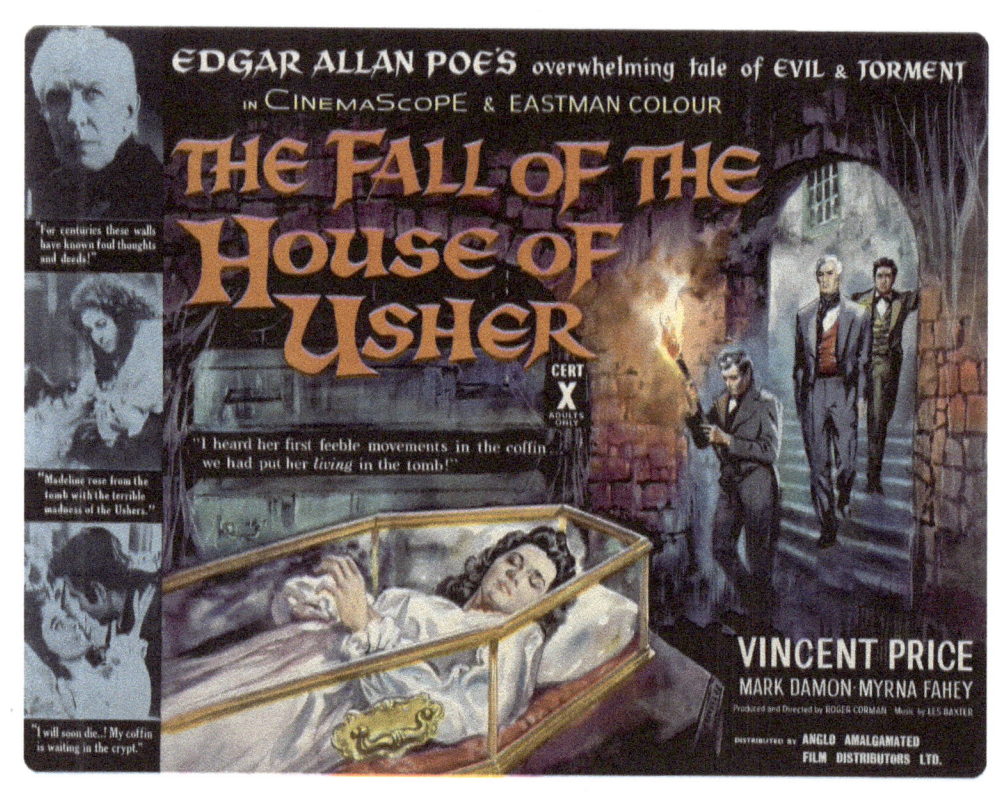

CAST
Vincent Price as Roderick Usher
Mark Damon as Philip Winthrop
Myrna Fahey as Madelaine Usher
Harry Ellerbe as Bristol

WRITTEN
Richard Matheson
Based on the short story
"THE FALL OF THE HOUSE OF USHER"
by Edgar Allan Poe

MUSIC
Les Baxter

CINEMATOGRAPHY
Floyd Crosby

EDITED
Anthony Carras

PRODUCTION DESIGN
Daniel Haller

SPECIAL EFFECTS
Pat Dinga

PRODUCED
Samuel Z. Arkoff (uncredited)
James H. Nicholson
Roger Corman

DIRECTED
Roger Corman

THE FALL OF THE HOUSE OF USHER

SYNOPSIS

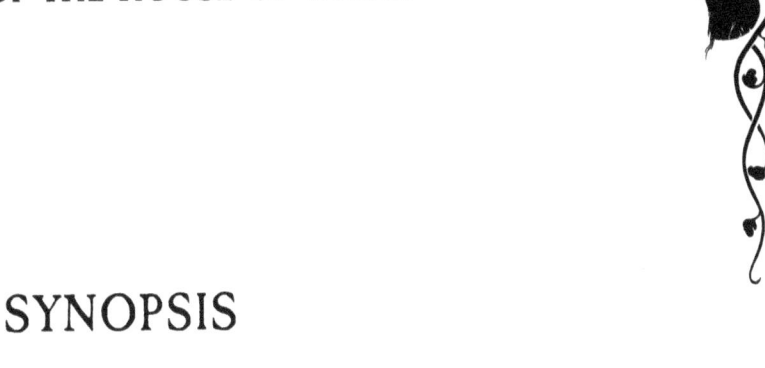

Dashing young Philip Winthrop winds his way through torched, mist-soaked forests towards the looming House of Usher, with romance on his mind. Philip had previously had a passionate affair with the lovely Madelaine Usher and the pair were engaged. However, after failing to hear from her, Phillip has grown concerned. His arrival at her ancestral home is met with anything but warmth as Madelaine's brother Roderick is aloof and almost immediately begs him to leave, citing his own tortured health condition that has rendered him painfully sensitive to light, sound and outside disturbances. Roderick also alludes to Madelaine's own all-consuming illness, one that ties both of their fates to his family's karmic curse, a legacy that has left them the sole heirs to the doomed Usher dynasty and — so Roderick believes — rendered them unable to ever leave the crumbling foundations of the house itself. Refusing to be swayed by these hyperbolic tales, Philip demands to see his lady love and insists on staying the night, secretly urging the despondent Madelaine to come away with him, despite her brother's apparent malignant brainwashing and her admitted bouts of uncontrollable sleepwalking. As one night becomes several, Philip begins to succumb to the gloom of the manor, with the house itself creaking and cracking and seemingly attempting to kill him. When Madelaine suffers a heart attack brought on by her alleged and unnamed condition, both Roderick and Philip tearfully mourn her passing and a hastily assembled funeral occurs. Later, when it is revealed that Madelaine in fact had suffered from clinically diagnosed catalepsy, Philip suspects she might have been buried alive. Against Roderick's pleading, Phillip breaks into the family crypt, tearing open his lover's coffin only to find it empty. Soon the corridors of the House of Usher echo with Madelaine's screams; the tormented woman was indeed intentionally entombed alive by her deranged sibling and is now hopelessly — and murderously — insane. The blood-covered, wraith-like thing that was once Lady Madelaine Usher attacks Philip, clawing at his face and inadvertently starting a fire. She then sets her now fully psychotic sights on her brother. As the damned siblings unite in a clutch of death and madness, the house burns around them and Philip narrowly escapes, standing before the blaze as it crumbles to ash.

"...and the deep and dank tarn closed silently over the fragments of the House of Usher." — Poe

INTERVIEW: ROGER CORMAN ON THE FALL OF THE HOUSE OF USHER

ALEXANDER: As a child, what was it about Edgar Allan Poe that first spoke to you?

ROGER CORMAN: I had read one short story — and that story was actually and appropriately "The Fall of the House of Usher"— as a school assignment in an English class. And it was the mystique of the story that got me: things happening on the surface but with something going on underneath. I didn't understand back then about subtext, but I was aware that something else was at play beneath the surface, which gave it a level of mystery and of a kind of horror that fascinated me.

ALEXANDER: So your love of literature was with you from this early age. Is this why, when you were working after high school at 20th Century Fox, you left to pursue a higher education?

CORMAN: Well, I left Fox after I had done some work on a script called THE BIG GUN, which was made into a picture called THE GUNFIGHTER with Gregory Peck. It was a classic Western and it was a big success. But I never got the credit for it; in fact, someone else got the credit, and I thought, "I don't want to stay here. I can see how this studio system works, I'm the low man on the totem pole and I can't see how I'm ever going to advance." And frankly, I had always wanted to go to Europe and I had time left on the GI Bill, so I applied to Oxford and was accepted there. That enabled me to go to Europe with the government paying my expenses as a university student.

ALEXANDER: Was your intention always to come back and re-immerse yourself in a film career?

CORMAN: Yes. But the idea was to stay one year, which is what I did, part of that time at Oxford and then the rest in Paris, where I lived the bohemian life on the Left Bank and came back knowing I wanted to work in films. I took various jobs. I was a literary agent for a while, then became a grip at a local television station called KTLA, then became an agent again and was writing all the way through that. I wrote a script and put another name on it, sold it and, to be fair, I paid the commission to the agency and told the head of the agency that I had written it in my spare time. It was a script called HOUSE ON THE SEA, and I told the producer that I would like to work for nothing as an associate producer to get the credit and learn. I knew if I could get the credits

THE FALL OF THE HOUSE OF USHER

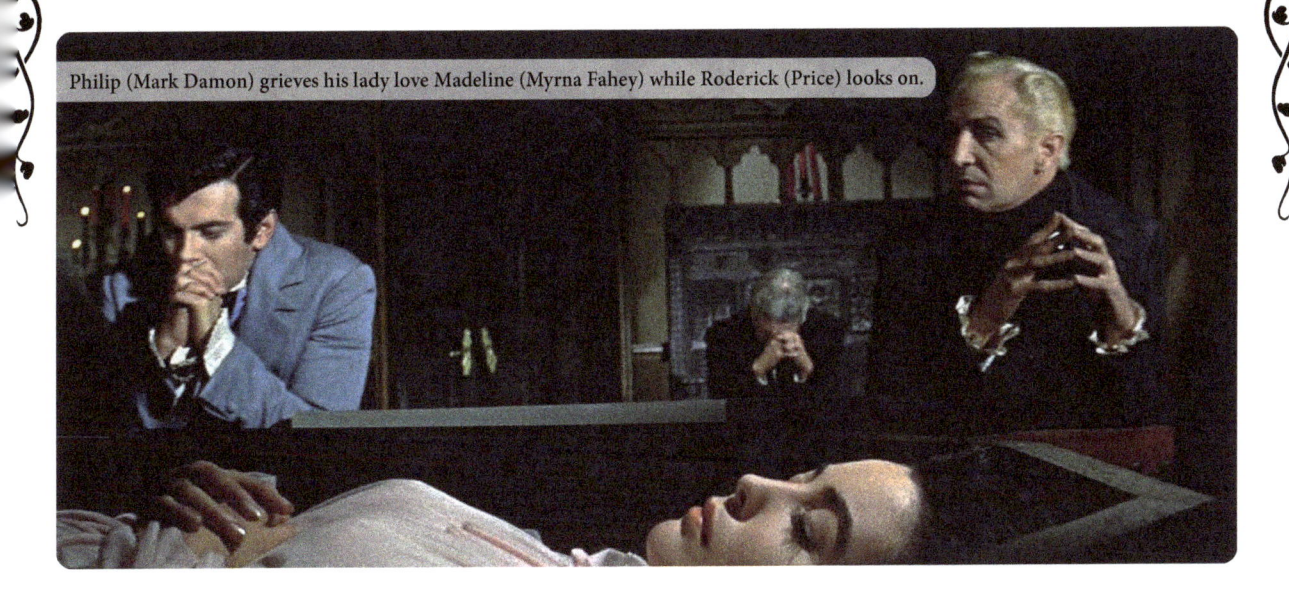

Philip (Mark Damon) grieves his lady love Madeline (Myrna Fahey) while Roderick (Price) looks on.

as writer and associate producer, I could strike out on my own.

ALEXANDER: You produced your first film, MONSTER FROM THE OCEAN FLOOR, in 1954, and very quickly after that became the producer and house director for American International Pictures. We know the stories about how, after making so many black-and-white fantasy films for AIP, you convinced James H. Nicholson and Samuel Z. Arkoff to invest in a pricier color picture; but why turn to the works of Poe at this point?

CORMAN: I wanted to step away from the contemporary horror films we were making and do a classic. As I mentioned, I had always loved "The Fall of the House of Usher" and I had always wanted to make a film version, so the idea didn't come out of nowhere. When this opportunity to make a more expensive picture arose, I pitched it to AIP and they accepted.

ALEXANDER: And Poe's work was also in the public domain.

CORMAN: Yes, it was.

ALEXANDER: So that was another consideration. How about the commercial success of the Hammer pictures out of Britain? Was that an influential factor in the creation of THE FALL OF THE HOUSE OF USHER?

CORMAN: No; weirdly enough, I didn't even know about the Hammer films. I hadn't even heard of the company until I went to England to do THE MASQUE OF THE RED DEATH several years later and people asked me about them. I saw one and thought it was a good picture, but I didn't even know they were in existence in the beginning.

ALEXANDER: In that fantastic first film, Vincent Price began his long, iconic union with you by starring as the tortured, possibly insane, Roderick Usher; it's a very controlled, almost subtle performance, especially compared to some of his other genre roles. Was Price also a Poe admirer?

CORMAN: I had a meeting with Vincent before we

Bristol (Harry Ellerbe) tries in vain to restrain a furious Philip.

made the picture and he certainly knew Poe's work, he'd read many of the stories, and we discussed the themes running through those tales, especially "Usher," and he took the role very seriously. He streaked his hair gray, almost blonde, acted with such gentle movements. He was very, very serious about the project. To him it was a classical role and he was in it all the way. I didn't want Vincent to play Roderick Usher as a monster. I wanted his intellect to be intimidating. If the audience was to fear him, I wanted him to be feared for his superior emotional sophistication and his intelligence, not for any sort of traditionally frightening aggression.

ALEXANDER: There's also the suggestion that there might be something sinister and incestuous between Roderick and Madelaine.

CORMAN: Yes, and that's something that Vincent alludes to in his performance. It's there on the peripheral just enough to add a sense of unease about not only Roderick but of the house itself.

ALEXANDER: And the house is the monster, or at least that's how you pitched it, correct?

CORMAN: Correct. When AIP read the script the first thing that they questioned was the absence of a monster. To them, a horror picture had to have a monster. I countered that by saying that the house WAS the monster and they bought that. When we were filming, Vincent had to say the line in the picture, something to the effect that "the house breathes". And he didn't quite grasp how to say it and asked me what his motivation was. I explained to him

THE FALL OF THE HOUSE OF USHER

how I had sold the concept of the house being the monster to AIP, and he immediately understood and then said the line perfectly.

ALEXANDER: Price's first appearance onscreen is a jolting one.

CORMAN: Yes, that was a deliberate technique, one I repeated many times in later Poe films. We created suspense with Mark and Harry Ellerbe walking down the hallway and just before Harry can knock on the chamber door, Vincent appears with a very fast entrance that gave the audience a bit of a shock. In fact, I was sure to create many smaller moments like this throughout the picture; brief shocks and jolts that would keep the audience alert and engaged, like the chandelier falling on Mark, or the railings of the staircase giving way. I had played with this building of suspense punctuated by a shock before in other pictures, but never as successfully as I did here.

ALEXANDER: And there's also that moment when Mark finds Myrna in the crypt…

CORMAN: Well, that was more of a big shock! That moment got a real scream from the audience, as did the shot where her bloody fingers emerge from the coffin near the end of the picture.

ALEXANDER: Price is, of course, the most recognizable face of the Poe cycle, but there is such a visual imprint on them as well, due in no small part to the work of art director Daniel Haller. Where did you meet him?

CORMAN: I don't remember exactly how I met Danny. We had worked on many pictures before Poe; he and I became friends, and I thought his work was simply better than any other art director I knew or had worked with. I stayed with him all the way through all the Poe pictures; he was the in-house art director for the series. I had a whole crew of people who worked with me from picture to picture; we all knew each other, and because of this we worked faster, more efficiently. Many of them became known as The Corman Crew, and often, when other producers went about hiring people to work on a film, they'd just say, "Let's hire The Corman Crew." It was like a good football team, really.

ALEXANDER: How did you assemble this crew? What was the criterion?

CORMAN: The way it was put together was this: on the first picture I made as a producer, I wrote down at the end of shooting, three columns. Column one was the guys who were good and I should hire back. The second column was guys who weren't very good and I should not hire back and the third column were guys who were just okay, but might be able to improve. So what I did on the next picture was hire back all the guys from the first column and about half of the guys on the third column, while also bringing on some new talent. And I did this on every film. So by the fourth or fifth film, I really had the best crew going for low budget films and they became known as The Corman Crew and they all took pride in the fact they

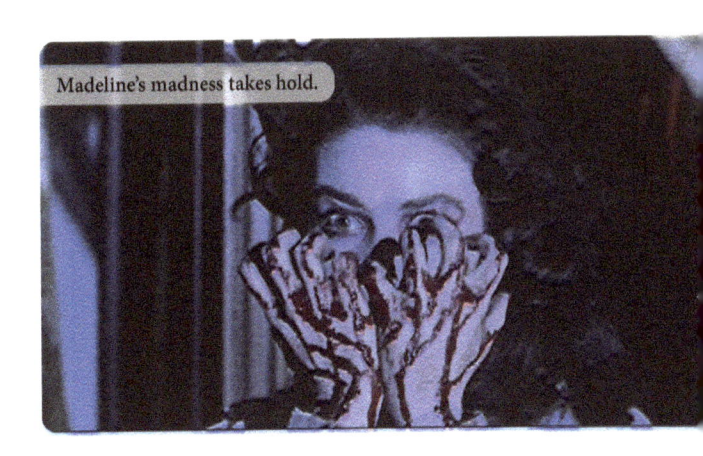

Madeline's madness takes hold.

CORMAN/POE

Lady Usher goes in for the kill.

were recognized as such.

ALEXANDER: And Danny was in that first column from day one?

CORMAN: Yes he was, right from the beginning and came back every time. In THE FALL OF THE HOUSE OF USHER, Danny filled the set with objects, paintings, statues, antique chairs and things that had detail, that were ornately carved. This added production value and in the wider frame, gives the audience more to look at, to let their eyes wander.

ALEXANDER: Speaking of paintings, Bert Shonberg's impressionist portraits of the Usher ancestors add so much to the almost surreal atmosphere of the film. How did you meet Bert?

CORMAN: Bert had a modicum of popularity at the time in the Hollywood post-beatnik, pre-hippie coffee house circuit and gallery scene and I remember him to be a very eccentric artist and an immensely talented one at that. I became aware of him and personally commissioned those paintings for the film. At the wrap, everyone took one of them home. I took Vincent's portrait and I still have it, in fact.

ALEXANDER: Did you tell Bert how you wanted the images to look?

CORMAN: Not really, no. He knew what to do and I understood his style. I think the distorted nature of the paintings works very well to mirror the distorted psychology of the Usher family.

ALEXANDER: It's tempting to cite Mark Damon's Philip Winthrop as the supporting role to Vincent's Roderick but I'm not so sure he is. How did you see it?

CORMAN: Mark is our initial point of entry into the story. He's a handsome, young outsider and the audience identifies with him as he becomes involved in this strange household. But I think — and this is credit both to Dick's script and Vincent's portrayal — that the audience also relates to Vincent, once we get to know him and understand him. They are drawn to his sensitivity and intellect and possibly see him as a sort of father figure.

ALEXANDER: How was Mark to work with?

CORMAN: Mark is a very good actor, in fact, and had a very interesting career. He started as a teen idol in America then went, like so many others did in the 1960s, to Italy where he became a star of westerns. He learned the language and ended up

THE FALL OF THE HOUSE OF USHER

becoming a prolific producer of European films and then returned to America where he became a very successful producer of Hollywood films. I like Mark very much.

ALEXANDER: And Myrna Fahey?

CORMAN: A very fine actress, a very beautiful actress. She came from "The Method" style of acting and had studied with Sandy Meisner and she was able to go from demure to frenzied effectively and enthusiastically. THE FALL OF THE HOUSE OF USHER was her first leading role and she went on to be a prolific television star.

ALEXANDER: Was composer Les Baxter considered part of The Corman Crew? His work on THE FALL OF THE HOUSE OF USHER is magnificent.

CORMAN: No, Les was suggested by Jim Nicholson. I listened to some of his work and agreed he would be good. We got along and he did some fantastic scores for me, and he was there throughout the process. I would give Les the script to understand the mood; then he would get the first rough cut so that he had an idea where we were going, and he'd start working on themes. We'd then show him each cut as we went along, and then, when we had the final cut, we'd send it to the Sound and Music Department — as we called it — so he could finish the score. All the sound effects were then laid out, so it would all come together at the same time.

ALEXANDER: The opening of THE FALL OF THE HOUSE OF USHER, with Mark Damon wandering towards the house is striking. It sets the tone of dread and decay to come.

CORMAN: Yes. That opening is a blend of a set, a matte painting and a real forest fire that occurred in the Hollywood hills that I had learned about after reading an article in the Los Angeles Times and seeing the accompanying picture of it. I was very determined to make this movie exemplify the unconscious mind, stemming very much from my interest in Freudian theory at the time, so THE FALL OF THE HOUSE OF USHER is primarily an internal, set-bound picture; almost as if we are in a contained, controlled, alternate reality. The shots of Mark in the surrounding forest were the only ones to show the natural world, albeit one we accentuated with the use of ground fog and lighting, which we then matched when he approaches the door or the house.

ALEXANDER: How long was the shoot?

CORMAN: It was — like most of the Poe pictures — shot in fifteen days, which was at that time the longest schedule I had ever worked with. And although lavish by AIP standards, the budget was still very low — about $300,000.

ALEXANDER: Did you have any time to rehearse with the actors?

CORMAN: We had only one day to rehearse and that was due primarily to the fact that American International Pictures didn't want to pay for anything above and beyond that. So we did a read through with the cast the day before the shoot and actually did that on the sets themselves, allowing us to quickly block out some of the action as well.

ALEXANDER: This was the first film that you shot in Cinemascope. How was that experience?

CORMAN: It was challenging. It was AIP that really wanted us to use scope and truthfully, I'm not sure we should have shot it in scope as this was — as I

The Usher siblings embrace one final time as the house burns.

mentioned — an interior picture, all on sets and not very big sets at that and cinemascope is best suited for wide open spaces and vistas. So we had to really be creative using wide lenses to create depth and I made sure to move the camera around quite a bit. There was so much dialogue in the picture that if we didn't create constant movement, I felt that we ran the risk of boring the audience.

ALEXANDER: And the man operating that camera was of course your regular man, Floyd Crosby.

CORMAN: Yes. Floyd was my cameraman on dozens of my films. Floyd had won the first every Academy Award for cinematography for a film called TABU, which was a picture he shot in the South Pacific. He was an extraordinary cameraman. Back then, you see, we called them cameramen, today they are referred to as cinematographers. At any rate, Floyd was semi-blacklisted. He wasn't really blacklisted but he was associated with some people who were blacklisted, so a number of studios would not hire him. But some studios would. For instance, he was the cameraman on one of the greatest westerns of all time, HIGH NOON. But most of the time, he was unemployed. I thought it was ridiculous. Here we have one of the best cameramen in Hollywood and no one would hire him. So I thought, why not, I'll call him up and see if he would like to be the cameraman on a low budget picture I was making and he said he was happy to do it. So, I used Floyd on the very first picture I directed — FIVE GUNS WEST, a western — and he was invaluable. Since I had never gone to film school, I had no training as a director, and he helped me very much in that first film. And then, as it turned out, on a majority of pictures we made, as you say, Floyd was always our go-to cameraman.

ALEXANDER: You mentioned that Sam Arkoff and Jim Nicholson at AIP insisted on having the picture shot in scope. But considering THE FALL OF THE HOUSE OF USHER was at that point one of their biggest investments, did they make any attempts to try to creatively control the movie?

THE FALL OF THE HOUSE OF USHER

CORMAN: No, quite the opposite in fact. They would show up on the first day of a shoot and walk around, meet everyone and then wish us well and you would rarely see them. The great thing about working with Jim — who was head of production, whereas Sam was in charge of the financial side — was that once we had an agreement on the leads, he stepped completely away. By the time we did USHER, I had been working with Sam and Jim for a few years and we had a very good relationship. And they were making several other pictures at the same time, so they were busy elsewhere. I had more freedom working with AIP than at any other company I have ever worked with.

ALEXANDER: Were the critics kind to THE FALL OF THE HOUSE OF USHER?

CORMAN: Yes, generally speaking, they were. In Europe, particularly in France, it was very well received, as were all the Poe pictures, especially in French film magazines like Cahier du Cinema, who, unlike most of the American critics, really took the time to read into the subtext of the picture. The film won several awards at various European festivals both for me and Vincent, with Vincent getting perhaps more of them than I did. THE FALL OF THE HOUSE OF USHER really was instrumental with establishing Vincent and I internationally and I would say that it was the movie that truly established AIP as a company.

ALEXANDER: What do you think it was about the film that really resonated with European audiences?

CORMAN: I'm not sure exactly, but I will tell you that although I say THE FALL OF THE HOUSE OF USHER was the picture that established me internationally, in France, I already had a following, which I learned about when they invited me to be part of a panel there. That fan base had started with a little ten-day gangster picture I had made called MACHINE GUN KELLY, which did very well in America but was incredibly popular in France. They loved it. And that's how the Europeans discovered this little-known actor named Charlie Bronson, who was — previous to MACHINE GUN KELLY — only a supporting player. After the success of my picture, Charlie was asked to do another gangster picture in Europe and then he spent the next few years playing in gangster films and westerns in Europe and became a huge star when he came back to the United States. So, to your question, I was already something of a name in Europe before the Poe pictures, but they established me more as director of note over there. Incidentally, they were even more popular in England and that's what partially led to me venturing to England to shoot both THE MASQUE OF THE RED DEATH and THE TOMB OF LIGEIA.

ALEXANDER: One of the signature style motifs of the cycle are those psychedelic dream sequences and I think that here, the first, is the most outrageous and frightening of them all.

CORMAN: You might be right and that's probably because it was indeed the first. The cast and crew loved doing it because we could put away the script and just invent something purely cinematic and almost expressionist. We distorted the lenses, played with lighting, experimented and the actors could be purely physical as there was no dialogue; the fantasy sequence is, in essence, like a silent film. And then we had great fun in post-production with printing and double printing and adding filters and voices on the soundtrack and we just went for it. In essence, as I say, an exercise in pure cinema.

ANALYSIS

That Corman and AIP's gearshift into more elaborate, sophisticated pulp filmmaking paid off with THE FALL OF THE HOUSE OF USHER is an obvious statement. But it did. As Roger cites, the film was commercially successful. But it's also a triumph of craft and unlike some of Roger's breezier pre-USHER efforts, it's a somber, deadly serious and genuinely upsetting experience. Everything just works, everything connects. From those opening moments, with the bursts of color-filtered fog swelling behind the credits while Les Baxter's thundering score builds on the soundtrack, to those unforgettable final moments of fiery mayhem and feminine madness, this is a strong, sensual and mature horror film. It's also one of the most literate of the Poe Cycle, second only perhaps to THE MASQUE OF THE RED DEATH, with a measured pace and endless dialogue exchanges that are as conversational and rhythmic as they are delightfully melodramatic and expositional and dripping with gravitas. And the performers are just as much to credit as the words written for them by the great Richard Matheson. Damon is, as many viewers and critics have cited, more or less one-note here, but that's by design. Philip is a one-note character; he's a man on a singular mission to rescue his lady love and push back against the perversity that engulfs her. It's a primarily functional and reactive role, a variation on Poe's nameless narrator in the original story, a character that serves as our point of entry into the Usher's mad world. In the source text, the narrator is in fact meant to be an old friend of Roderick's who comes to visit, a narrative device that would have served a screen adaptation just fine, pushing the horror and mystery angle. But would have robbed it of any sort of dramatic urgency. In Matheson's more romantic remounting, it's Philip's all-consuming love for Madelaine that not only draws him to the house, but keeps him — and therefore, us — there. It's passion and reason that vies for control over Roderick's unhealthy, illogical and borderline (or maybe, as some, including Roger have suggested, slightly more explicit) incestuous obsession with his sister. And yet both men are unwavering in their virtue, both believe themselves to be right. And both are more than a little bit self-serving, mutually wanting to "save" Madelaine. It's Madelaine who is the real victim here, a pitiful creature who has been in effect robbed of any sort of free will by the overpowering males who surround her. And the house? It's simply

THE FALL OF THE HOUSE OF USHER

Roderick listlessly strums his broken notes as Philip scowls.

the apathetic observer to these histrionics. The house is in fact nothing more than nature itself, no more of a monster than the elements, than the desolate, barren woods surrounding it. A mirror of the atrophied state of the family: old, outdated, forgotten by time and deeply, irrevocably sick. All of this subtext of course comes from Poe's mind, but is amplified here by Matheson, fleshed out by Damon, Price and Fahey and brought to vivid, visual life by The Corman Crew. It's a horror film, certainly, and a terrifying, sensational one at that, both in its Freudian ideas, its dank, morbid mood and its final act splashes of bright red blood against white skin and wide eyes. There are images here that are truly unforgettable, and every moment just feels slightly off and kind of…curdled. Even sequences of Roderick listlessly strumming atonally on a lute creep under the skin and stay there, especially when Philip inexplicably praises his macabre, sour sonata. Everything is just wrong.

Comparisons to Terrence Fisher's Hammer horror films of the time are appropriate on a surface level, despite Roger's claims that he had never seen one prior to production. But unlike those early Hammer Gothics, whose scripts rarely delved too deep into what Roger calls the "subconscious mind", USHER is a bubbling cauldron of repression, psychological and sexual abuse, mental illness, death and the crude banalities of human evil.

THE PIT AND THE PENDULUM

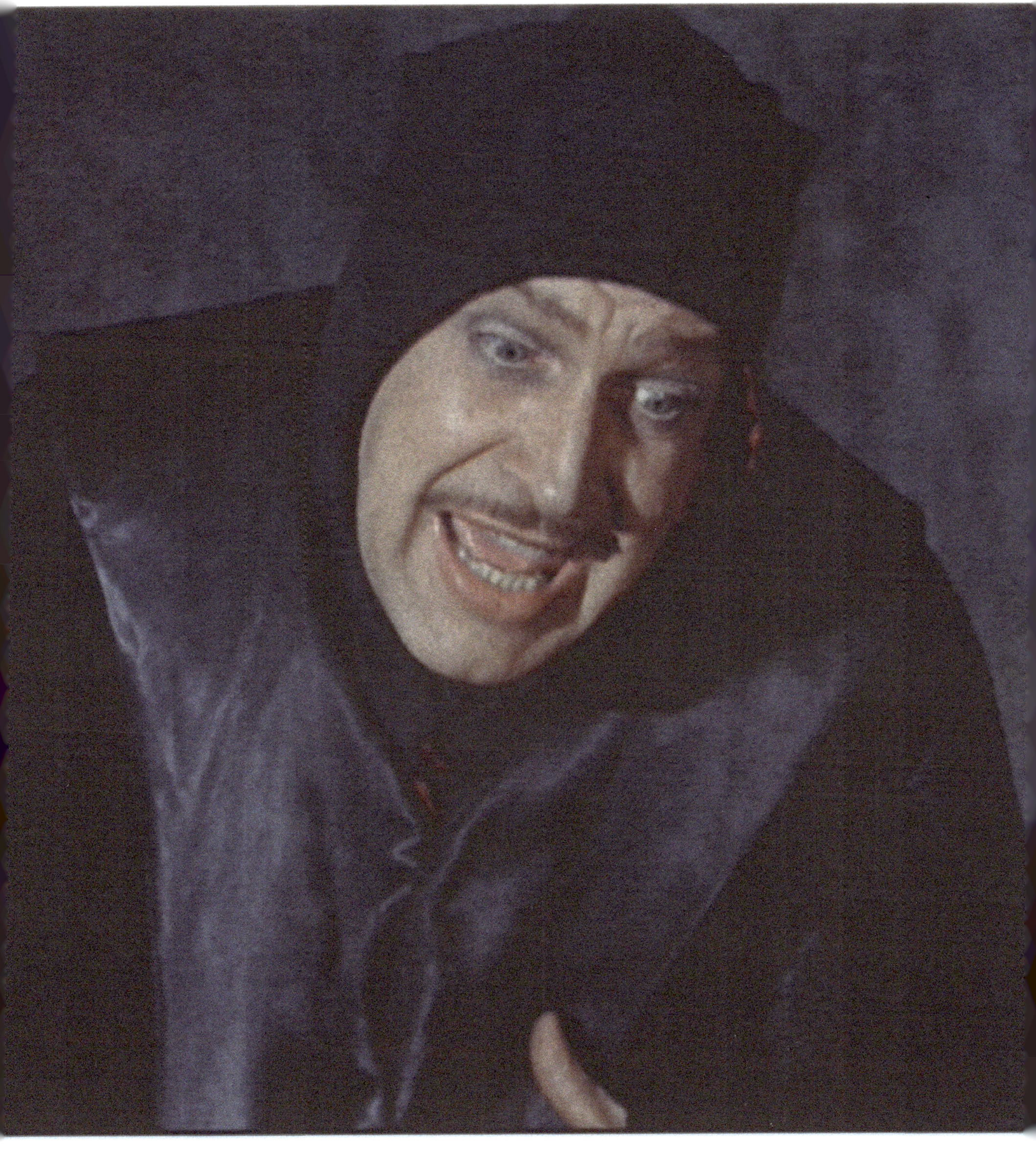

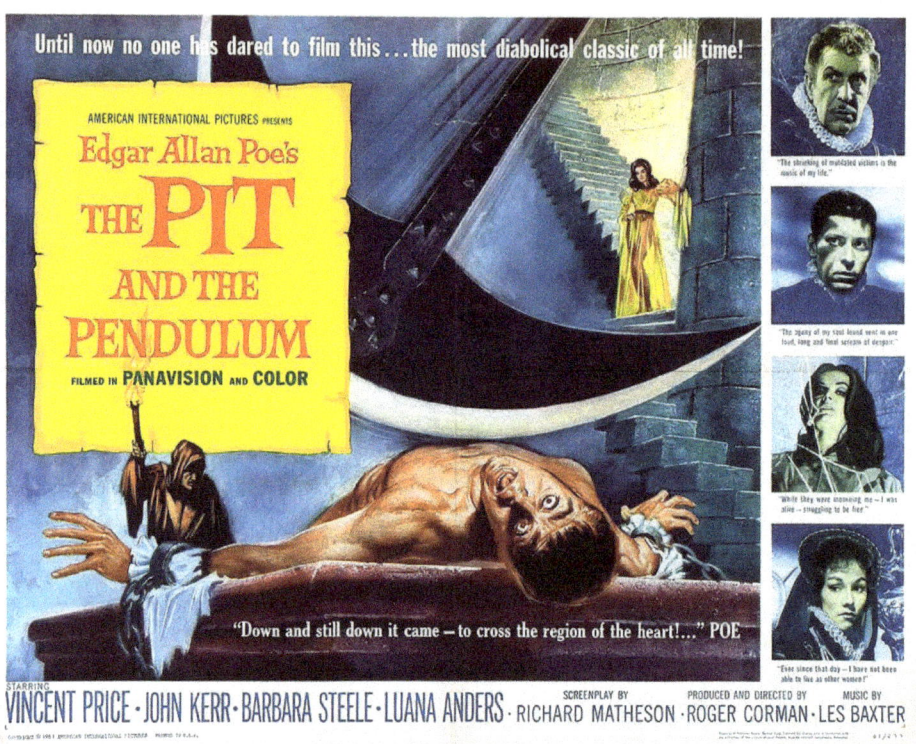

CAST
Vincent Price as Nicholas Medina / Sebastian Medina
John Kerr as Francis Barnard
Luana Anders as Catherine Medina
Anthony Carbone as Dr. Charles Leon
Barbara Steele as Elizabeth Barnard Medina
Patrick Westwood as Maximillian

WRITTEN
Richard Matheson
Based on the story "THE PIT AND THE PENDULUM" by Edgar Allan Poe

MUSIC
Les Baxter

CINEMATOGRAPHY
Floyd Crosby

EDITED
Anthony Carras

PRODUCTION DESIGN
Daniel Haller

SPECIAL EFFECTS
Pat Dinga

PRODUCED
Samuel Z. Arkoff
James H. Nicholson
Roger Corman

DIRECTED
Roger Corman

SYNOPSIS

Traveling to Spain in the wake of his sister Elizabeth's recent death, Englishman Francis Barnard arrives at the coastal castle belonging to her husband, Nicholas Medina. Despite being told by both Nicholas and his sister Catherine that Elizabeth died of a rare ailment, Barnard refuses to accept their hazy claims and instead insists on staying at the house until he can investigate further. It soon becomes clear that Nicholas is feeling the pain of Elizabeth's loss far worse than anyone and has become a tortured shell of a man, riddled with guilt that he himself is responsible for her untimely passing. When Dr. Leon, Elizabeth's physician and family friend comes to call, he informs Barnard that his sister did not in fact die of any sort of sickness, but rather suffered a massive heart attack, likely brought on by some sort of shock. His ire and suspicion aroused anew, Barnard demands more information from the Medinas. Nicholas reluctantly obliges and quietly takes him down to the bowels of the castle, to the spot where Elizabeth was found dead. The basement houses a dilapidated torture chamber, a relic of the Spanish Inquisition and a place that, according to Nicholas, Elizabeth had become obsessed with, vanishing for hours, fixated on the gruesome instruments of pain and misery rotting within. After becoming increasingly distant and melancholy, Elizabeth apparently went down into the chamber one final time, accidentally locking herself in an iron maiden, the final words on her lips "Sebastian", the name of Nicholas' late father Sebastian Medina, himself a notorious figure in the inquisition. Later, Elizabeth delves even deeper into the history of the chamber, explaining that as a little boy, her brother was playing in the room when his father, mother and uncle entered. The wicked patriarch, suspecting the pair of adultery, proceeded to kill his brother and then, while the hiding child looked on, tortured his wife to death.

As Nicholas continues to emotionally unravel, strange noises begin plaguing the household at night — whispers, knocks, a ghostly harpsichord — leading the increasingly unhinged Nicholas to believe his dead wife still walks. Dr. Leon justifies this paranoia by explaining to Barnard that both he and Nicholas believe that Elizabeth may in fact have been entombed alive and that her spirit may indeed be haunting the house. The disturbed Nicholas demands the crypt be smashed open so he himself can see his wife's corpse and, when the coffin is exhumed, they

CORMAN/POE

Nicholas Medina (Price) paints while his wife Elizabeth (Barbara Steele) plots.

find Elizabeth's desiccated body, its mouth open and frozen in a scream, its hands clawed and broken from scratching on the casket lid. Nicholas reels back, now teetering on the edge of sanity as his worst fears are verified. Later that night, when Nicholas hears his dead wife's voice calling to him, he follows it down the steps back towards the crypt only to be surprised by the image of Elizabeth, vibrant and healthy. He falls back in shock as Elizabeth is joined by Dr. Leon, the pair having been secret lovers who had hatched an elaborate scheme to drive Nicholas insane once and for all. As Elizabeth cruelly taunts the now catatonic Nicholas, gloating over the irony that his mother was an adulteress and now his own wife has made him a cuckold, something snaps in the mad nobleman and he pulls himself out of his stupor, a sinister, leering look upon his face. Nicholas has now taken on the persona of his dead father Sebastian and, believing in his delirium that Dr. Leon is his uncle and Elizabeth his mother, attacks them, killing Dr. Leon and dragging Elizabeth screaming into the torture chamber.

Hearing the shrieks, Barnard runs down to investigate only to find Nicholas now fully dressed in the black robes of the Inquisitor. Nicholas strikes Barnard, knocking him out and then proceeds to tie him to a stone slab. When Barnard wakes up, he discovers that the raving Nicholas has activated the dreaded pendulum device, a swinging blade that is slowly lowered with the end goal being to hack its prey in half. As the gears of the pendulum grind and Barnard struggles in vain to free himself, Catherine and her servant Maximilian burst into the chamber, Maximilian pushing Nicholas into the pit while Catherine struggles to stop the pendulum. She does, and the weary heroes exit, Catherine proclaiming that "no one will ever enter this room again". The door behind them slams shut and is locked, much to the horror of the gagged Elizabeth, who is still trapped in the iron maiden, her eyes wide in horror knowing full well that she is now doomed.

"...the agony of my soul found vent in one loud, long and final scream of despair" — Poe

INTERVIEW: ROGER CORMAN ON THE PIT AND THE PENDULUM

ALEXANDER: THE PIT AND THE PENDULUM has a very similar setup and narrative drive to THE FALL OF THE HOUSE OF USHER; was this an attempt to duplicate a successful formula on yours and Richard Matheson's part?

CORMAN: It wasn't an attempt to duplicate a formula per se; rather, it was an attempt to replicate the themes of Poe. We were working with one man's vision, after all, so there was a consistency that permeated all of Dick's scripts for my films. Remember, most of these scripts were built out of stories which were very short, so we had to isolate the essence of Poe's stories and elaborate on them.

In THE FALL OF THE HOUSE OF USHER, we had Mark Damon walking through a burned out forest in the Hollywood hills. Here, we have John Kerr arriving on the beach, with the ocean behind him, very symbolic as the water is where we all come from. We filmed that at the Palos Verdes coast, by the way. A very striking spot.

(L-R) Luana Anders as Catherine Medina, Vincent Price as Nicholas Medina and Anthony Carbone as Charles Leon.

CORMAN/POE

Terror rises from the tomb as Nicholas faces his fears.

ALEXANDER: Matheson hated when filmmakers tinkered with his scripts and has often noted that you were one of the few directors that never did.

CORMAN: That's true. I myself have changed scripts heavily during shooting, but I don't think I ever had to change anything substantial with Dick's work, maybe a couple of lines here and there, maybe not. His scripts were so right-on, I shot them 95 percent exactly as they were — and I say 95 percent because no one ever shoots a script 100 percent. Dick was one of the finest writers I've ever had the chance to work with and I credit him for much of the success of those early Poe pictures.

ALEXANDER: One notable element of THE PIT AND THE PENDULUM is that Matheson structures the story as a supernatural mystery. The audience believes they're watching a ghost story until that third act.

CORMAN: Agreed. It's an illusion. In THE FALL OF THE HOUSE OF USHER, any feeling of the supernatural is just that, a feeling. Here, the audience is kept guessing wondering if Elizabeth Medina is haunting her husband. But in both cases, Dick followed a formula of using Poe's original story as the third act and building a story around it, as a road to lead us to that story that Poe wrote. You could think of it in some ways as Dick and I creating a prologue for that story.

ALEXANDER: Another thing that is interesting here, as in almost all the Poe pictures, is that you don't specifically date the pictures. There's no explicit mention of time or place.

THE PIT AND THE PENDULUM

CORMAN: I didn't feel it needed that. It's an interior film, a fantasy and I felt the film stood for itself with historical elements present enough — in this case, mention of the Spanish Inquisition — without pretending the story was in any way anything else but a work of fiction.

ALEXANDER: Price's work in THE PIT AND THE PENDULUM rides completely off the rails in the double role; a brilliant, fearless performance. Did you ever have to reel him in?

CORMAN: Sometimes. I would talk to him and use that word again, "interior," and that meant he had to use an interior motion when he acted. It never happened on THE FALL OF THE HOUSE OF USHER because he knew exactly what the role would be. But after USHER, he became more aware that we were making horror films, as opposed to the classic picture we made the first time. The word "classic" may have faded slightly with THE PIT AND THE PENDULUM, and the concept of horror began to grow.

ALEXANDER: And it truly blossoms when he both plays his own father in flashback and then assumes the persona of his father in the climax!

CORMAN: Yes. Vincent adopted a limp and specific look in his eye and lilt to his face to illustrate not only a different character but a truly evil one. Vincent really was a brilliant actor and I think he delivered a fully realized emotional performance.

ALEXANDER: Floyd Crosby really created a visual identity with these films—all those ghostly blues and violent, sexual reds.

CORMAN: The blue was all Floyd, but the reds, particularly the red candles, were my contribution. I like foreground composition, and you know, as I said those sets were not very big; Danny did a great job of building these incredible sets for very little money and I liked the idea of red candles burning in the foreground and shooting beyond them. In fact, the joke was that I had used up all the red candles in Hollywood!

ALEXANDER: That melting paint in the pre-credits, coupled with Baxter's ominous music is abstract and terrifying.

CORMAN: I've always believed that having a strong opening serves to really grab the audience's attention and draw them in. For the opening of THE PIT AND THE PENDULUM, we actually had those flowing liquids and double printed them and then used Les' music to build and set a mood, something psychological and almost atonal, I think.

Corman directs while Elizabeth shreds what's left of Nicholas' sanity.

Floyd Crosby notes the demands of his director while Steele stays in character.

ALEXANDER: You cast the great Barbara Steele in a pivotal role as the villainess. Barbara has such a great look and a great speaking voice, which you opted to dub. Why?

CORMAN: Well, first of all, Barbara is a wonderful English actress and a very striking one, with those incredible cheekbones and eyes. There was a slight weird, or mysterious, quality about her. She was at that point very popular in European films and I had seen Mario Bava's BLACK SUNDAY, which I admired very much. So we actually moved her name up in the opening credits to help in European markets. So we brought her over to make the picture and to my surprise she had this working class, this almost low class level accent and we had to try to work with her to refine that accent. Ultimately, we had to dub her voice with another actress' voice simply because her accent wasn't working and didn't lend itself to the character. I think by this time she was used to having her voice dubbed by other actors in her European films.

ALEXANDER: I've always liked seeing Anthony Carbone perform in your films. He's got this great urgency and gravitas in THE PIT AND THE PENDULUM; the character is sort of the grand orchestrator of everything, manipulating everyone and everything around him.

CORMAN: Tony was a very good, very intense, thoroughly trained method actor and I understood how he was working. I appreciated the "Method" and I didn't have to really direct Anthony, he just knew what to do and made the role his own. I never could quite understand why he didn't have a bigger career. He worked steadily as a character actor, but never really hit the way he should have hit.

ALEXANDER: You also worked often with Luana Anders, an incredibly talented performer, writer and producer. What are your memories of Luana?

CORMAN: My relationship with Luana goes back to when I was very seriously trying to train to be a better director and ties in to how I met Anthony as well, and that was all centered around the "Method." I felt that since my degree from Stanford was in engineering, that I learned how to use the camera and picked up all the technical aspects of being a director fairly quickly, but I realized that I didn't have enough knowledge to work with actors. So I enrolled in Jeff Corey's class. There were a number of acting teachers at the time and he was the leader of the Method school in Los Angeles and I realized, coming out of the actors' studio, that this style was where everything was heading. So I enrolled in that class and I met a number of people, including Tony, Jack Nicholson — who I felt was the best actor in the class — and Bob (Robert) Towne who was a great performer and eventually a very talented writer. And both of them, of course, would end up working for me. But I thought Luana was the best

THE PIT AND THE PENDULUM

THE PIT AND THE PENDULUM swung into U.S. theatres on August 23rd, 1961.

Elizabeth smiles knowingly at her lover as the hapless Nicholas makes merry.

actress. She didn't quite have the look to be a standard, beautiful leading lady. But she was an excellent actress and I used her often because she was just so talented. And yes, as you say she was successful in many ways. Years later, she actually wrote a script for me called FIRE ON THE AMAZON which was Sandra Bullock's first picture that I shot in Peru.

ALEXANDER: Some have cited John Kerr's performance in THE PIT AND THE PENDULUM as wooden. I disagree and feel his performance is consistent and pitched just right for the material.

CORMAN: I would agree and I was very pleased with his work. John was a very interesting actor. He got his start as a leading man on Broadway before coming to Hollywood and much later, left the business entirely to pursue medicine and became a doctor.

ALEXANDER: In THE FALL OF THE HOUSE OF USHER, Bert Shonberg painted nightmarish portraits of the Usher lineage. In THE PIT AND THE PENDULUM, the paintings on the wall of the Medina home are much more realistic. Was this by design?

CORMAN: I wanted the film to have a bit of a different look, something more opulent as this was the house of a nobleman, and that went for the paintings as well. I felt at the time that they suited the picture better. In retrospect, I much prefer Bert's work in USHER, as it was wholly unique and impressionist and worked better for the picture. It's a case of trying to change things and not repeat yourself and then admitting that your instincts were correct the first time around.

ALEXANDER: I've heard you mention before that the castle in THE PIT AND THE PENDULUM,

THE PIT AND THE PENDULUM

with its corridors and catacombs, was meant to be feminine, almost vaginal.

CORMAN: Yes, because I was then still very, very much into studying Freud and believed in many Freudian theories about the unconscious mind, maybe more than any of my contemporaries were. I thought of both the house in HOUSE OF USHER and the castle in THE PIT AND THE PENDULUM as representative of a woman's body and the front doors of which were metaphorically speaking a vagina, yes. The character enters and then spends time moving down corridors and up and down staircases in ways in which, to me, were very sexual. The audience watches the character moving through that corridor and gets tense, anticipating something. They want the character to retreat but at the same time want them to go forward and find out what's at the end of that corridor. And then of course, we hit them with a shock or scare and that provides a kind of release, which is very much akin to sex. Of course, most people in the audience won't consciously make that connection and that's fine if they don't.

ALEXANDER: Instead of the traditional fantasy sequence that marked the Poe films, here the more experimental sequence is in fact a flashback, a story being told. Was this sequence a more controlled one to shoot as opposed to THE FALL OF THE HOUSE OF USHER's more go-for-broke approach?

CORMAN: I wouldn't say more controlled; perhaps it feels that way because the sequence is more based in reality. But the approach was the same in that we used a variety of lenses and experimented with lighting and filters and performance styles in order to slightly distort things. I also used a very early cinema technique of opening and closing the iris to bring us into the sequence. And when we come out of that sequence and return to reality, I adjusted the contrast somewhat, so things were slightly brighter to really make the audience feel the switch.

ALEXANDER: You used scope photography here again. Were you more comfortable with it this time around?

CORMAN: I would say so, yes. And we filled the screen with even more detail than we had in THE FALL OF THE HOUSE OF USHER and ensured there was constant movement with the camera and within the frame. I will again credit Floyd Crosby for teaching me all about scope photography in USHER. I had understood a bit about it, simply by pure logic, but Floyd filled in all the blanks for me and by the time we got to THE PIT AND THE PENDULUM, I had a much firmer grasp on it. I owe that all to Floyd.

ALEXANDER: The design of the dungeon is astonishing. One of Haller's finest creations.

CORMAN: That was partly a matte painting shot matched with a smaller set. The background was actually the wall of the soundstage. The pendulum was constructed with wood and metal and the blade was made of rubber, if I recall correctly. I believe we had another blade for close-ups which was a very sharp metal blade and then used the rubber one when it was swinging in the scenes with John. Today, that matte painting would have been done using CGI effects and it would be more realistic, but I think for what it is, it's incredibly effective and still holds up.

ALEXANDER: Was John Kerr comfortable strapped underneath that swinging horror?

CORMAN: No! When we were setting it up, attaching the blade above the set and test swinging

CORMAN/POE

Elizabeth's obsession with the Medina torture chamber swells.

it as it lowered onto the platform where John was to be strapped, John came up to me with a very worried look on his face and said "Roger, do you think that thing is safe? I'm a bit worried about getting under there". And I thought, great, that's all I need — an actor who doesn't want to get under the pendulum when that's the title of the picture! So I said, "John, there is no problem at all with any of this. It's absolutely safe. Look, I'll get under it." And they started swinging that giant pendulum back and forth and it was getting closer to me and I'll admit that I was thinking that, yes, perhaps this was NOT such a safe stunt after all! But it turned out just fine. The grip stopped it just before it was about to hit me and that convinced John to play the scene as written.

ALEXANDER: The entire finale is harrowing, a master class in editing as well as design and performance.

CORMAN: And the audience really reacted to that ending. As soon as they saw that pendulum hanging, they gasped. We cut back and forth between Vincent, the pendulum, Luana outside the door and John tied up under the swinging blade and then back to the matte shot to give a sense of the scope of it all. The intercuts to the paintings on the wall were all comprised of shots I took during the last hour of shooting, just before we went into overtime or, as it is called, "Golden Time" and I got on a crane with the camera and Floyd and I just shot anything on the set that looked good. I didn't have a plan, but I figured that I would make sense of it later, in the edit. And I did and it worked well.

ALEXANDER: When THE PIT AND THE PENDULUM had its initial run on television, it featured an elaborate, bizarre opening prologue featuring Luana's character, Catherine Medina. I've heard varying accounts as to who actually directed that piece, either yourself or your assistant.

CORMAN: Yes, it was me who directed that. When the picture was finished, it was a little bit too short to fit into the standard timeframe of a television broadcast. So I directed that opening, but it was a different thing. It was this sort of add-on sequence that we had to make up to pad it all out. I didn't want to do anything that would break into the picture because I felt that the picture stood on its own. So I thought, I'll just supply them with a new opening and that way, it will function as an introduction of sorts to the central story. In it, Luana is in a kind of asylum, and she is tormented by the inmates into telling her story, which ends up being the feature film. I shot that prologue in one day and really, I wasn't pleased with it at all. But it was all right for what it was, and it served its purpose. But the film works far better without it, in my opinion.

THE PIT AND THE PENDULUM

ANALYSIS

The opening moments of THE PIT AND THE PENDULUM are some of the most dramatic and primordially terrifying I've ever experienced in any horror film. On the most obvious level, all Corman shows us is melting, oozing liquids gushing into more liquids, pulsing in every direction. And yet the effect is pure dread, especially when accentuated by Les Baxter's reverberating, percussive and dissonant score. This is psychedelia before there really was a trend of psychedelia in pop art. And that in and of itself is interesting because Corman would spend plenty of time experimenting with more explicitly psychedelic material later in his career when he made the move into more contemporary, youth culture films like THE TRIP and GAS-S-S-S. Of course, the filmmaker had elements of more dream state, subconscious and surreal imagery in THE FALL OF THE HOUSE OF USHER, but nothing as boldly minimalist as this. It's a sort of manifesto to open a horror picture this way, a suggestion that the world we are about to enter is one that is unstable, amorphous; as if the gushing juices are madness itself, perhaps exemplifying the state of mind of the tortured Nicholas Medina. Or maybe of the general sickness that Medina's grim dynasty has birthed and the fates that await each and every player we're about to meet because of that dynasty. Or maybe it's meaningless, just a visually interesting, abstract way to begin Corman's symphony of horror. No matter the motive, it's an unforgettable curtain riser.

That startling, ominous prologue dissolves into a shot of our hero traveling by coach along what is meant to be the Spanish coast, the waves crashing against the rocks at the foot of the towering fortress he moves toward as the opening credits dissolve into frame and those Baxter-orchestrated plucked strings and deep drones continue on their nightmarish path. Of course, this is familiar turf, a quote on Matheson's opening for USHER but replacing the brittle burnt woods with the anger and almost erotic force of the ocean.

And that set up isn't the only thing the two pictures have in common. In both, our protagonist is on a mission, investigating the fate of a woman close to him; in THE FALL OF THE HOUSE OF USHER it's a mission to liberate a lover from doom and here it's an attempt to find out why a sibling met her demise. And in both of course, the patriarch of the house is a tortured soul, teetering on the edge of sanity (and both roles are of course essayed by Vincent Price).

But the mechanics of these mutual entry points aside, THE PIT IN THE PENDULUM is a very different beast. As Corman himself suggests, USHER was a careful attempt to blend the literary with the sensational whereas PIT is a full blown, albeit finely tailored, horror film. And I think it's not only the best of the Poe cycle, but perhaps Roger's best film too, a wild and dramatic freefall into mania and perversion made with an edge of genuine experimentalism, black as night humor and untouchable craft. A bona fide masterpiece of Gothic horror and kinky psychodrama that never loses an ounce of power upon multiple rewatches.

As an aside — and one I debated addressing in this book — in my long history with THE PIT AND THE PENDULUM, I once came across a video interview with THE FALL OF THE HOUSE OF USHER star Mark Damon, located on the back end of Anchor Bay's DVD release of Mario Bava's BLACK SABBATH (in which Damon co-stars), wherein he states that he in fact actually directed PIT. I was shocked, to put it mildly, as was every other Corman admirer who stumbled upon this odd chat. For one, I had never heard or read anything to back these claims up from any other source close to the production. And for the other, it threw off my entire Corman confirmation bias. If I was citing THE PIT AND THE PENDULUM as Roger's crowning achievement, and he didn't actually direct it, where would that leave me? Not being one to let things go, I tracked down Damon, who indeed is now a revered producer, a career shift that evolved once he ventured to Italy — like so many American B movie stars did — to find fame in European genre films. Damon bartered his career as a star of Italian westerns to eventually have a creative role on set, and in some cases direct some or all of the films themselves, something he also claims he did with 1972's wonderful sexploitation shocker THE DEVIL'S WEDDING NIGHT. I asked Damon about these statements, and he sort of back-peddled on them, telling me that he had in fact "brought" the Poe properties THE FALL OF THE HOUSE OF USHER and THE PIT AND THE PENDULUM to Corman and told him he would star in the first picture as long as he could direct the second, to which Corman agreed. This didn't sit well with me for a few reasons. For one, the collected work of Poe is now and was then in the public domain.

THE PIT AND THE PENDULUM

Even if Corman's account of admiring Poe as a youth was exaggerated, his higher education in English literature would ensure that he was acutely aware of the ubiquitous author's work. For another, Damon was a name at the time, but certainly not a huge name and his marquee value wasn't enough for Corman to be inspired to agree to any such deal. Besides, it was AIP calling the shots as to who would be directing what and when in those days, not Corman. When I pushed this issue, Damon told me that because of this, Corman had to keep their deal quiet and that Damon actually directed the actors — not the action — uncredited.

Unsatisfied, I brought this up later that year when I was chatting with Roger about the re-release of one of his pictures on home video. As soon as I mentioned Damon's claims, Roger did a double take and asked me what on earth I was talking about. He vehemently — but with his usual class and restraint — denied that Damon had anything to do with THE PIT AND PENDULUM at all and suggested that Mark might be "somewhat confused".

Sometime later, I spoke with European horror icon and PIT co-star Barbara Steele, who was friendly with Damon during their mutual professional and social encounters in Italy during that wonderful period in the 1960s, and also asked her about Damon's insistence that he had been at least partially responsible for directing PIT. Unlike Corman, Steele didn't hold back. Starting with a laugh and then countering that with indignant outrage, Steele flatly stated that no one but Roger Corman directed her or anyone else on that set and that Damon — who she didn't even remember visiting the set — was and always would be "a lousy raconteur". Later still, I would hear from others who knew Damon socially and listened to both this and other odd anecdotes of films he had claimed some responsibility for. I'm satisfied that, for whatever reason he chose to tell it, Damon's account of the making of THE PIT AND THE PENDULUM is utter nonsense.

THE PREMATURE BURIAL

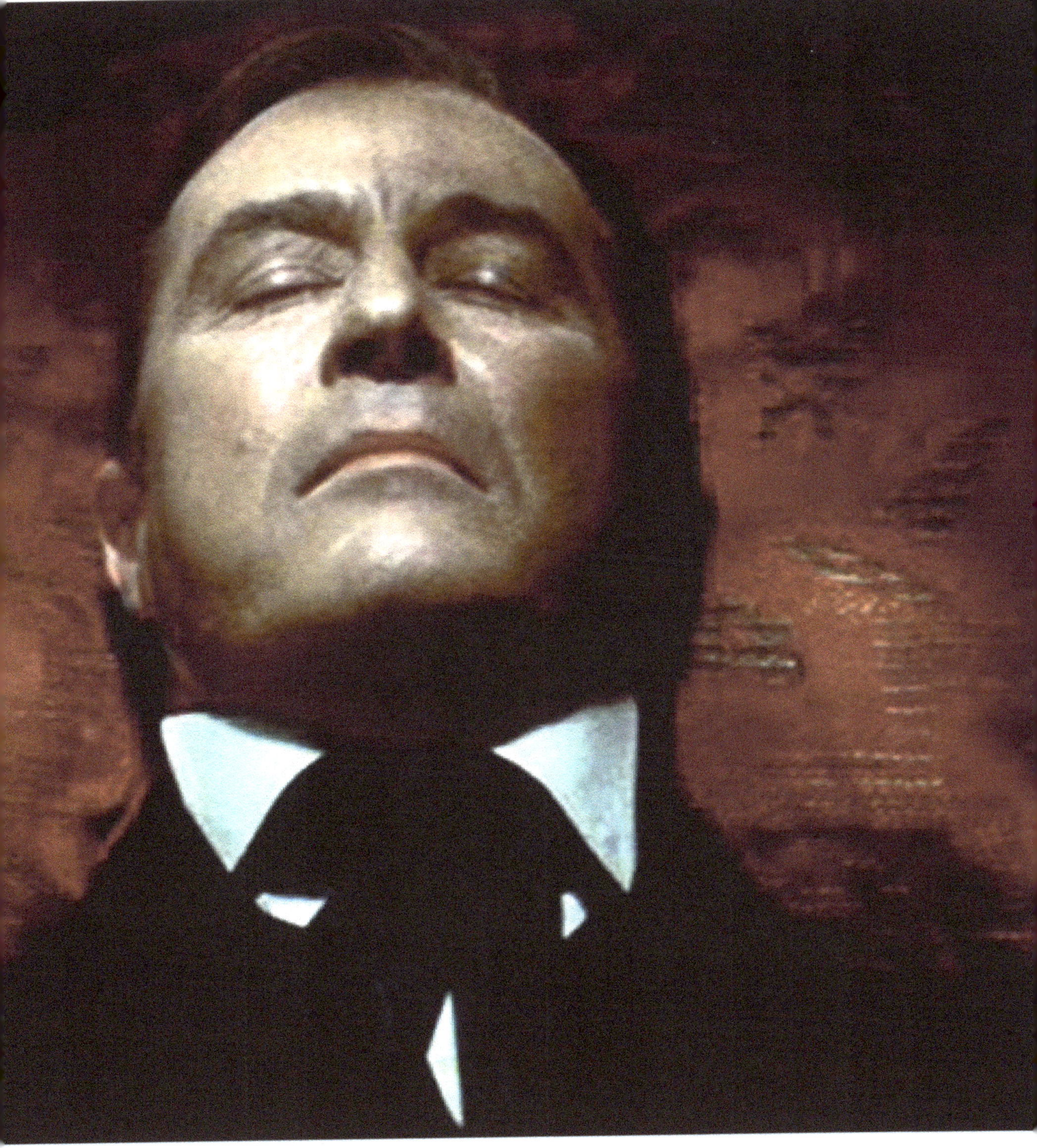

CORMAN/POE

CAST
Ray Milland as Guy Carrell
Hazel Court as Emily Gault
Richard Net as Miles Archer
Heather Angel as Kate Carrell
Alan Napier as Dr. Gideon Gault
John Dierkes as Sweeney
Dick Miller as Mole
Clive Halliday as Judson
Brendan Dillon as Minister

WRITTEN
Charles Beaumont & Ray Russell
Based on the story "THE PREMATURE BURIAL"
by Edgar Allan Poe

MUSIC
Ronald Stein

CINEMATOGRAPHY
Floyd Crosby

EDITED
Ronald Sinclair

PRODUCTION DESIGN
Daniel Haller

SPECIAL EFFECTS
Lou LaCava

PRODUCED
Samuel Z. Arkoff, James H. Nicholson,
Roger Corman & Gene Corman

DIRECTED
Roger Corman

THE PREMATURE BURIAL

SYNOPSIS

Aristocrat Guy Carrell stands in watch as a pair of ragtag graverobbers toil at their trade, exhuming a coffin from the earth, all the while one of them whistling the old English folk tune "Molly Malone". When the lid of the box is removed, Guy notices what looks like bloody claw marks on the interior of the wood. He immediately gasps in horror and as the camera pans down, we see why: the desiccated corpse's mouth is open in what looks like a frozen scream. The man has clearly been buried alive.

Sometime later, Guy's estranged fiancé Emily comes to visit. It seems he has called off their engagement without explanation and has instructed his sister Kate that he doesn't wish to even see his former love. But Emily is adamant and pushes her way in, confronting Guy in his study. He begs Emily to leave, to forget she ever met him and claims that he is damaged goods. He explains that as a boy, he heard his father screaming in the family crypt, entombed alive, though no one, not even his sister, believed his tales. Guy's father suffered from catalepsy, a condition that now plagues him, his mounting paranoia of being buried alive consuming his every thought. Undaunted, Emily refuses to leave Guy's side and insists they continue with their nuptials. She promises to stand by his side and help him navigate his isolating anxiety and mental health issues.

The pair wed later that month, and, during the reception, Emily sits at the piano and begins to play "Molly Malone", much to Guy's horror. He insists she never, ever play the tune again and Emily reluctantly agrees. At night, Guy hears what sounds like a scream and, walking into the fog-drenched night with his sister, finds his dog dead on the moors. When the animal suddenly revives, Guy's obsession with premature burial deepens.

As the months pass, Guy and Emily have still not had a honeymoon, and when their mutual friend Miles comes to visit we learn why. Refusing to be a victim of his condition, Guy has devoted his days to building an above ground crypt, one meant only for him. He excitedly demonstrates his ingenious device, one which comes complete with a collapsible coffin equipped with chisels and hammers and a bell that can be rung to get help should he accidentally be entombed alive. And if all his tricks should fail, a goblet of poison sits waiting in a shrine, a guarantee of his successful demise. None of this sits well with Emily, who vows that she will leave Guy unless he abolishes his morbid obsessions and devotes his window, the haunting whistling sounds of "Molly Malone" drifting out of the ether…or is it only in his mind? As Guy's mental state deteriorates, Miles insists that they open the family crypt to prove that Guy's father was not in fact buried alive; however the shock of what he sees sends Guy into a state of shock and he collapses. Though actually suffering from the very catalepsy he feared, his doctor states that he has had a heart attack and declares him legally dead. Emily is devastated and expresses her wishes for Guy to be buried in the cemetery as opposed to the crypt. As his coffin is lowered into the ground, Guy, now paralyzed but very much awake and aware, lives the very terror he feared and is buried alive.

Later, the graverobbers dig him up, with the intention of selling Guy's corpse to the doctor for medical experimentation. Awake and now completely insane, Guy bursts out of the coffin and murders the graverobbers, disguising himself as one of them to gain access to the doctor's examination room and then quickly dispatching him as well. Believing that his wife is also guilty of a plot to prematurely bury him, Guy drags the screaming Emily to his own now open grave and roughly tosses her in, shoveling dirt onto her terrified face just as Miles interrupts the gruesome scene and attempts to stop him. Guy overpowers Miles and just before he kills the younger man, Kate appears and shoots Guy dead. Miles reaches for Emily and pulls her from the grave, but it's too late. As Miles mourns her and tries to make sense of the horrors he has just witnessed, Kate tearfully explains that she had been on to Emily from the start and that Emily was in fact trying to use Guy's fears to either drive him insane or kill him, thus inheriting all of his wealth. As Miles and Kate walk away from the grave, we pan back to the eerie final image of Guy and Emily, husband and wife, lying broken beside each other, united forever in death, their tombstone etched in the epitaph "Rest in Peace".

his attentions to her and their marriage. The ultimatum works and Guy soon burns down his custom-made crypt, telling both his wife and friend that he's seen the light and is ready to get back to the business of living.

But almost immediately, the fragile-minded man begins having visions of the filthy graverobbers from the opening of the picture appearing in the woods, at

INTERVIEW: ROGER CORMAN ON THE PREMATURE BURIAL

ALEXANDER: You had a temporary falling out with AIP after THE PIT AND THE PENDULUM, which led you to do THE PREMATURE BURIAL without them. What happened there?

CORMAN: There was a little problem — as there always is between filmmaker and distributor — over the percentage of profits and what deductions should be taken. So I decided to do THE PREMATURE BURIAL on my own. Now, I should also mention that AIP was by and large — and especially in comparison to other studios — a very honest and forthcoming company. But there were still some issues between us. Pathe Labs, who we had worked with for many other pictures, were starting their own distribution company and we agreed to do THE PREMATURE BURIAL together, with both of us agreeing to put up half of the money. So production pushed forward until, on the morning of the first day of shooting, Jim and Sam came to the set and graciously shook my hand and wished me all the best on making the picture. I thought this was strange, but ultimately a very nice gesture on their part, as if to say that business was business and they still genuinely wished me well. But then Sam said — through a bright smile — that they had just bought out Pathe's backing and that THE PREMATURE BURIAL was going to be an AIP picture after all!

ALEXANDER: You say this with a smile on your face today, but you must have been furious initially.

CORMAN: Actually, I don't think I was particularly angry really. I remember that I just kind of smiled at the entire thing and thought that, in fact, it was really rather a clever move on their part. I had a bit of reluctant respect for them for doing that.

ALEXANDER: Why didn't you continue with the signature of the series and cast Vincent Price in the role of Guy Carrell?

CORMAN: I couldn't go with Vincent initially because he was under exclusive contract with AIP for that type of Gothic film, which was a brilliant move on Sam's part, as he understood Vincent's value in these pictures. So I chose Ray Milland instead, who I admired very much.

ALEXANDER: What are your feelings on Milland's work when you watch the film today?

CORMAN/POE

Guy Carrell (Ray Milland) demonstrates his escape tomb while Emily (Hazel Court) and Miles (Richard Ney) stifle their shock.

CORMAN: I think he was very, very good. He brought a slightly different feeling to the film. Both Vincent and Ray had been Hollywood stars, but Ray was — if you will — a brighter star in his time, in that he was more famous and had won an Oscar for THE LOST WEEKEND. Vincent was a character lead; Ray was a true romantic lead and very handsome. I think the role in THE PREMATURE BURIAL actually fit Ray a bit better than it would have Vincent.

ALEXANDER: And you worked with Ray again the following year in X: THE MAN WITH THE X-RAY EYES.

CORMAN: I did, which I also think was a very good picture and I think Ray was perhaps even better in it, though it's a very different film and hard to compare the two. Originally, I had Ray's character imagined as a scientist, but I thought that had been done too many times. So I went with the idea of a Jazz musician — as I was always something of a jazz fan — who takes a new kind of drug that gives him the power to see through things. But when Ray became involved I changed the character into a doctor who is experimenting with ways to improve vision. Ray was perfect for it.

ALEXANDER: You also went with different writers for THE PREMATURE BURIAL in Charles Beaumont and Ray Russell, the latter who also co-wrote X.

CORMAN: Yes and I'm not sure why I did that originally. I think Dick Matheson wasn't available at the time, it must have been that. But that was all fine and good because Chuck and Ray along with Dick were also part of that same group of writers in Hollywood at the time, who were writing very similar

THE PREMATURE BURIAL

types of science fiction and fantasy books, stories and screenplays. They were all friends and they all had a very similar quality about their writing and were all excellent writers so I was very comfortable using all of them.

ALEXANDER: Both you and Richard have said that Matheson's first drafts for your pictures were usually shot verbatim. Was it the same with Beaumont and Russell?

CORMAN: If I'm to be honest about it, no, it wasn't quite the same. While yes, Chuck and Ray were, as I mentioned, excellent writers, I felt that the script for THE PREMATURE BURIAL was not quite as effective as Dick's work had been on THE FALL OF THE HOUSE OF USHER and THE PIT AND THE PENDULUM and I do recall changing some things.

ALEXANDER: With a new star and new writers, did your approach to directing THE PREMATURE BURIAL differ much from the previous films?

CORMAN: Generally speaking, no. My directing style remained basically the same. Ray and Vincent were certainly very different screen presences as I mentioned, but both were complete professionals and very easy to work with

ALEXANDER: What are your memories of Hazel Court? THE PREMATURE BURIAL marks her first appearance in the Poe cycle.

CORMAN: Hazel was wonderful, both on set and on the screen. She had a certain quality, a kind of sophistication and intelligence. She was a trained British actress and had by this point already appeared in a few horror films and had relocated to America. She added a theatrical quality to the film and elegance. And she was a total professional. And yes, I used her for two more Poe pictures after that, with THE MASQUE OF THE RED DEATH being perhaps her best performance in the series, although she was also very good in THE RAVEN.

ALEXANDER: It's also nice to see Dick Miller appear here, in a small but important role as one of the dastardly gravediggers. Dick was in so many of your films and yet this is the only one of the Poe pictures he was cast in.

CORMAN: And I can't recall why that was, exactly. It might have had to do with his general presence, which was always best suited to more contemporary pictures. Dick was a dear friend. There was no one quite like him. He was very flexible and a master improviser. A very talented and very funny man.

ALEXANDER: How were the box-office returns for THE PREMATURE BURIAL without Price's presence on the marquee?

CORMAN: They all did about the same, roughly. If I recall right, THE PIT AND THE PENDULUM was the most successful. But AIP did very well with all of them.

ALEXANDER: You're a scholar of European and art-house cinema, and when you quote, say, the work of Ingmar Bergman, it is clear. But in those fantastic, distorted dream sequences in the Poe films, specifically here in THE PREMATURE BURIAL, there are echoes of the surrealist sensibilities of Luis Buñuel and Salvador Dalí. Were you inspired by the surrealist movement at all?

CORMAN: Yes. I loved the works of Buñuel, who was one of the greatest directors of all time, and had of course seen many of Dalí's paintings. There were

ALEXANDER: You have discussed at length your interests in and influence of Freudian theory in the first two Poe pictures. Do you feel THE PREMATURE BURIAL is reflective of those theories as well?

CORMAN: To a degree, yes, absolutely. The explorations of the unconscious mind and the setting of the action primarily on sets in fabricated interiors. That's all there. But I was also developing my own theories based on other books I was reading on psychology, with the driving theory being that terror or horror is really just the psychological re-creation of childhood fears and fantasies. When a child is alone in their dark bedroom at night and they hear thunder and wind and rain, they become very frightened as these are forces they do not understand and they have very limited ways in which to cope with them. A parent can soothe them by saying that "It's only thunder or it's only lightning" to help normalize these things. But that only goes so far. These experiences mark a child deeply, I think. And I think the ways in which we react to horror and the unknown in film is simply a revisiting of those times in childhood. Because of these theories I was investigating at the time, I think I made more of a direct effort to make THE PREMATURE BURIAL even more of a horror picture than the others.

ALEXANDER: So you do think that horror pictures are, as many have said, a form of catharsis for the viewer?

CORMAN: In a way, I suppose, they can be. The horror film exposes those ingrained fears and identifies them. And they strike a nerve because most of us raised in a traditional Western way have had common shared experiences and anxieties and

no direct, intentional references in the Poe films to either of their works, but the ideas within them inspired me, absolutely.

THE PREMATURE BURIAL

respond to uniform provocations. Sometimes we aren't even conscious of them but I think the horror film can draw them out.

ALEXANDER: One of the strongest impressions THE PREMATURE BURIAL leaves on the viewer is the whistled theme that permeates the film, "Molly Malone".

CORMAN: Yes. One thing I realized very early on is the importance of sound in a horror picture. Not just in horror films actually, but in any and all films. What you hear can be just as important as what you see and of course, sound can amplify the way you react to what you see. I think the use of sound is a very important element in all the Poe pictures, but I would say in THE PREMATURE BURIAL I was much more aware of its use. Both the whistling in the fantasy sequences and the even more subtle uses of it throughout really add to the feeling of horror. As I said, with THE PREMATURE BURIAL I was very focused on amplifying the horror.

ALEXANDER: All of the Poe films deal with characters who are on the fringes in some way. Various types of "outsiders" who are isolated, either by their actions or by events out of their control. I find Guy Carrell to be perhaps the most alienated of them all, with maybe Verden Fell in THE TOMB OF LIGEIA a close second. Do you have an inherent interest in this kind of character?

CORMAN: I would say to a large extent, yes. Not just in the Poe films, mind you, but in many of my films you'll find characters like this.

ALEXANDER: Do you think of yourself as an outsider?

CORMAN: You know, in some respects I do. Though I've generally always had a place in the mainstream, I've always felt somewhat outside of it. In my films, I'm very interested in capturing a spirit of rebellion against authority, against the establishment; it's about fighting back against being given orders and perhaps seeking a deeper truth.

ALEXANDER: Ultimately, how do you personally feel about THE PREMATURE BURIAL in relation to the other Poe films?

CORMAN: I'm very pleased with it. And I watched it again recently with an audience and was very happy with how it's held up. It has a bit of a different look and texture, not just because of the casting of Ray, but there's a mood to it that sets it apart, I would say. It's true that it doesn't seem to get the same contemporary attention as some of the other Poe pictures do and I attribute that primarily to Vincent's absence. But I certainly think it's a fine picture.

ANALYSIS

As Roger states, contemporary consensus on THE PREMATURE BURIAL (or as its title appears onscreen, simply and inexplicably, PREMATURE BURIAL) is that it is indeed a lesser entry in the Poe Cycle. And that's unfortunate. Certainly, Ray Milland is a much more muted presence than Vincent Price and perhaps because of that very reason, the movie is a considerably more somber affair. But Milland is actually perfect for the part of the perpetually miserable, cynical and hopelessly claustrophobic protagonist. He has a wounded look, his eyes nervously darting back and forth from his rounder face and his often rude demeanor masking the barely controlled hysterical terror within. Whereas Price is a master of the grand gesture and operatic emoting, Milland has a functioning "inner voice" that runs constantly under writers Beaumont and Russell's scripted words. It's a masterfully controlled performance, really, embedded in a weird, tight, kinky and hyper-Gothic exercise in death obsession.

The familiar tropes established with Corman and Matheson's first two pictures are all here: the melancholy, barely controlled antihero; the feminine presence who may or may not have ulterior, sinister motives; mist-soaked exteriors, exhumed coffins with mummified, prematurely interred corpses within and a frenzied climax where everything and everyone descends into abject lunacy. And yet THE PREMATURE BURIAL feels very much independent of the series; something unique, dramatic and laced with dark humor. And though Milland plays it rail straight, he's definitely in on the sick joke. The sequence where the unhinged Guy Carrell gleefully demonstrates the various features of his wacky custom escape-room crypt is brilliant and grimly hilarious, with Milland jumping excitedly from device to device to his ultimate fail-safe, while his wife and best friend look on, their astonished jaws — and ours — virtually scraping the floor.

Corman's sense of macabre atmosphere is at its apex here. Whereas THE FALL OF THE HOUSE OF USHER oozed sensual menace and THE PIT AND THE PENDULUM pushed the envelope on Grand Guignol, THE PREMATURE BURIAL just sort of slinks around with a kind of snarling menace, slowly, methodically working its way along its path to a tragic, almost cruel finale. I don't think

THE PREMATURE BURIAL

Guy's all-consuming anxiety of being buried alive become a grim reality.

it's a particularly frightening film, but it's moody, psychologically ripe, intelligent and consistently engaging. And it sticks with you long after the final end title rolls.

Hazel Court marks her first of three Poe Cycle appearances here and admittedly the script doesn't really give her much to do save for looking lovely and being a sort of cipher that propels Guy's journey along. Unlike Barbara Steele in PIT or Myrna Fahey in USHER, Court's last-act turn into femme fatale villainy doesn't really register and is mostly explained away in Kate's expositional closing monologue. Still, Court's Emily is a sensuous presence, and her liquid vivaciousness plays beautifully against Milland's emotionally distant rigidity. THE PREMATURE BURIAL also marks composer Ronald Stein's debut in the cycle, and it's a majestic, masculine score, as opposed to the lush, romantic, sometimes even experimental orchestrations Les Baxter laid upon USHER and PIT. Stein ingeniously marries his music to the whistling grave robber (the great Dick Miller, here credited as Richard Miller) in the film's opening, the tune "Molly Malone" weaving its way in and out of the music and later, the plot itself, in various ways, making it a sort of character. It's colder and more clinical than Baxter's work but it perfectly suits and accentuates the film.

TALES OF TERROR

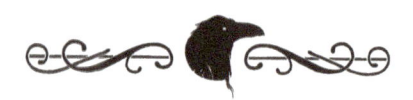

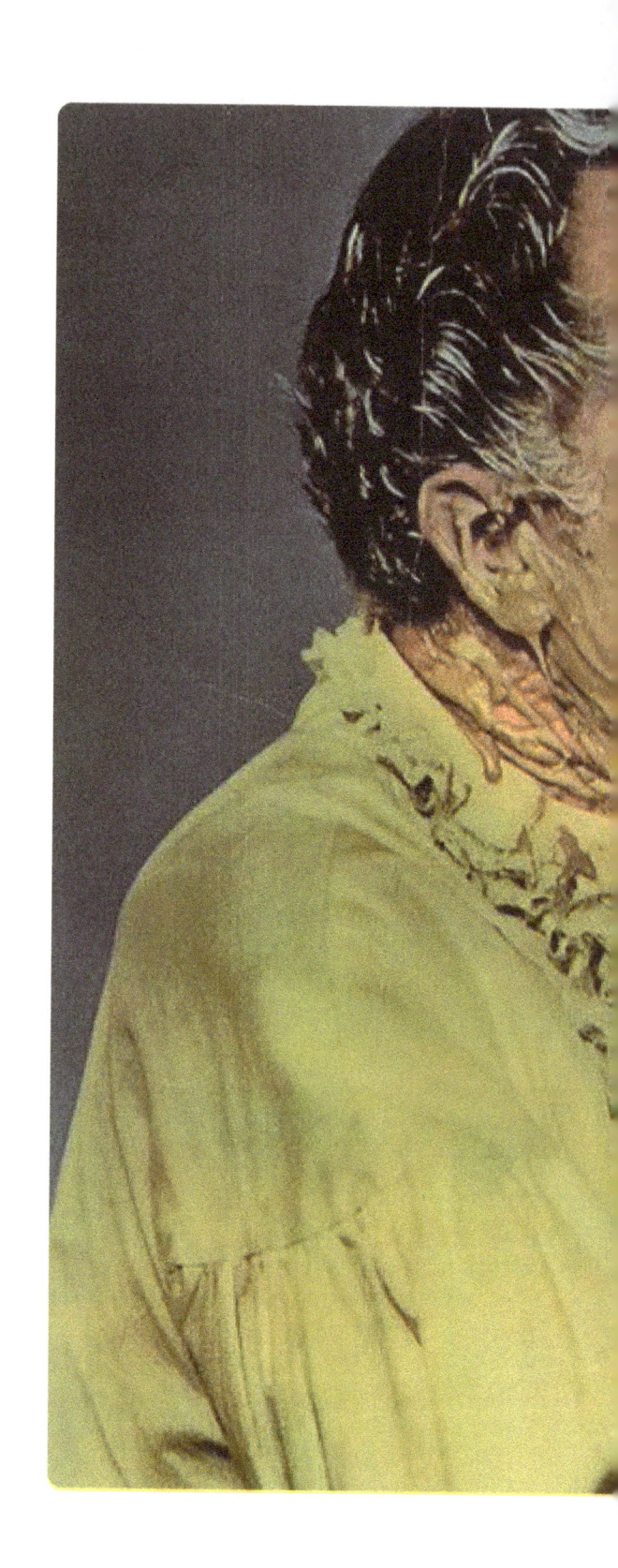

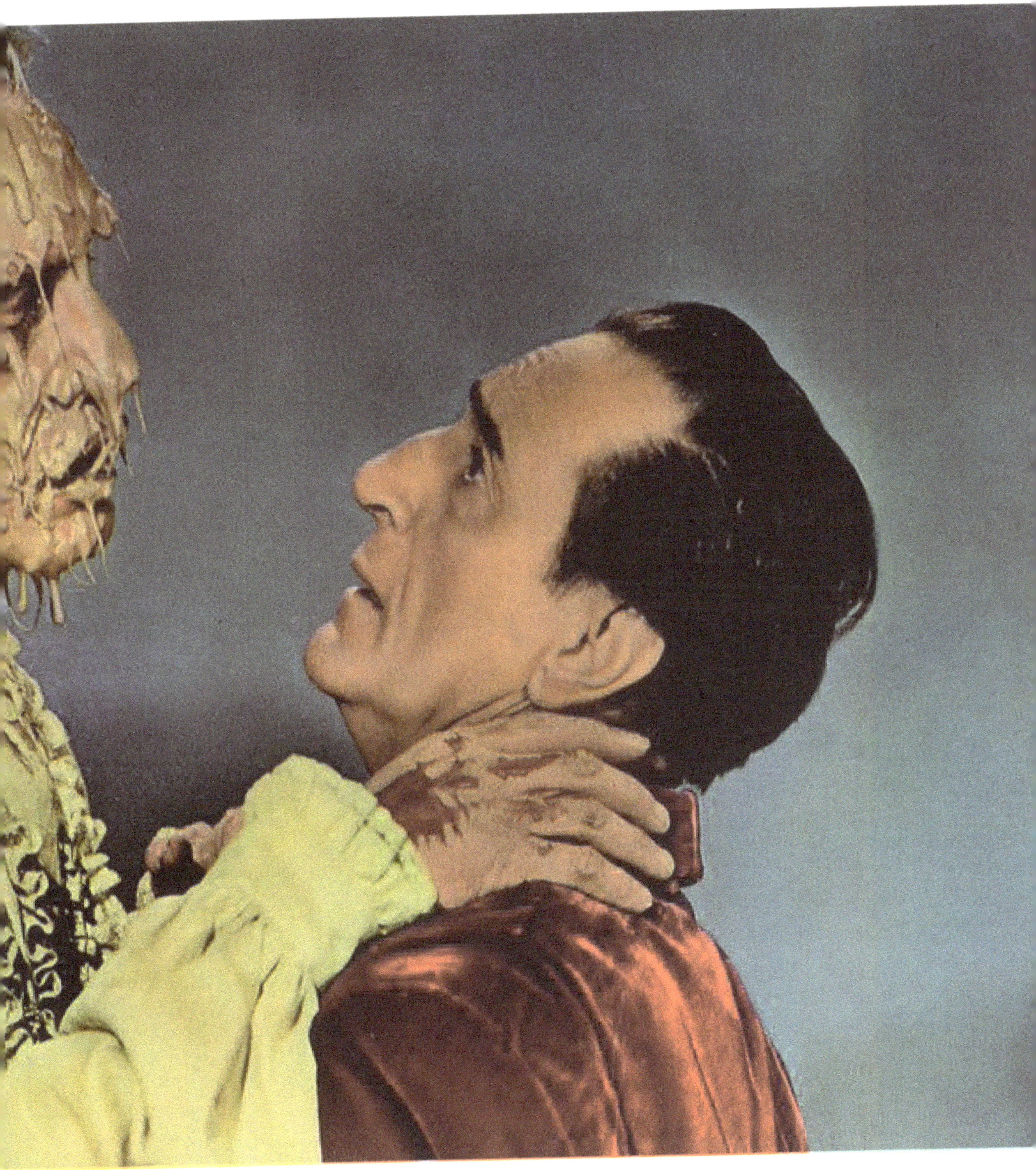

CORMAN/POE

CAST
"Morella"
Vincent Price as Locke
Maggie Pierce as Lenora
Leona Gage as Morella
Edmund Cobb as The Driver

"The Black Cat"
Vincent Price as Fortunato Luchresi
Peter Lorre as Montresor Herringbone
Joyce Jameson as Annabel Herringbone
Lennie Weinrib as Policeman
John Hackett as Policeman #2
Willy Campo as The Barman
Alan DeWitt as The Chairman on the Wine Society

"The Case of M. Valdemar"
Vincent Price as Ernest Valdemar
Basil Rathbone as Carmichael
Debra Paget as Helene
David Frankham as Dr. James
Scott Brown as Servant

WRITTEN
Richard Matheson
Based on the stories "MORELLA", "THE BLACK CAT", "THE CASK OF AMONTILLADO" and "THE FACTS IN THE CASE OF M. VALDEMAR" by Edgar Allan Poe

MUSIC
Les Baxter

CINEMATOGRAPHY
Floyd Crosby

EDITED
Anthony Carras

PRODUCTION DESIGN
Daniel Haller

SPECIAL EFFECTS
Pat Dinga

PRODUCED
Samuel Z. Arkoff, James H. Nicholson
& Roger Corman

DIRECTED
Roger Corman

TALES OF TERROR

SYNOPSIS

As an ominous narrator speaks on the nature of death and dying, a beating human heart strobes on screen. We dissolve into a painting of a coastal mansion; a Gothic tableaux that comes to life as the first of three "tales of terror" begins.

"MORELLA"

A horse drawn carriage travels through a fog soaked forest, stopping at the door of a house. Its passenger is Lenora, a young woman who is returning to what is her family home, apparently after a long absence. She finds the building interior in disrepair, webs upon webs coating corners and furniture, dust settled thick on every surface. As Lenora walks the home's creaky staircase, she is surprised by the man she's come here to find, her father, Locke, who now, like the house, is unkempt and rundown. At first the apparently inebriated patriarch doesn't recognize his daughter and when she identifies herself as such, his already cool demeanor drops a degree. Annoyed by her presence, Locke begrudgingly

Carmichael (Basil Rathbone) reveals his brutish nature after he's spurned by Helene (Debra Paget).

agrees to his daughter staying the night; when she adjourns to her suite, he turns to face the portrait of a beautiful, raven haired woman. "Morella, my beloved wife," he says, "your murderer has returned."

Later that night, Lenora explores the house's many rooms and wanders into one in particular in which a bed sits, covered in a filthy, shredded canopy. Lying upon the bed lays the desiccated body of Morella, the woman from the painting and Lenora's long deceased mother. Lenora's shocked scream causes her father to run in, furious that anyone — let alone Lenora — is anywhere near the body of his dead wife. As Locke pours another drink, his tone softens and he explains that Morella died in childbirth and his ensuing misery and mourning manifested itself as a hatred for his infant daughter, blaming her for his lost love's demise. Lenora tearfully tells Locke that she is suffering from a terminal illness, with very little time left to live, and that her trip to the home was solely to make peace with the man who gave her up so many years prior. Locke, seeing the cruelty of his ways and feeling a wave of guilt and regret, embraces his daughter and pleads for her to stay with him for what's left of her life.

That night, Morella's spirit wakes and vows revenge on her daughter, her "murderer". Her translucent form drifts down the corridor into Lenora's room and melts into her body, causing Lenora to suffer a heart attack. A tearful Locke pulls the bedsheets over his child's face, lamenting that he wishes he could join her in death. But when he hears moans coming from beneath the shroud, he pulls it back and is shocked to see Morella in her place, very much alive and well. Running from the room in horror, he finds his daughter's corpse lying in his wife's shrouded bed instead and, jumping back, accidentally knocks a candle to the ground, the flames immediately catching and climbing the walls. Behind him, Morella closes in, wrapping her hands around his throat while the house burns. In a final pair of shots, we see that it is now Lenora who lies dead on top of Locke's strangled body.

Back in her death-shrine lies Morella, a wicked, satisfied grin stretched across her mummified face.

"The winds of the firmament breathed but one sound within my ears and the ripples upon the sea murmured evermore…Morella." — Poe

"THE BLACK CAT"

Stumbling from a tavern, after yet another night of boozy indulgence, Montresor Herringbone heads home, out of money and out of his mind drunk. His long-suffering wife Annabelle greets him, now apparently very used to this routine, which includes her loutish husband tearing apart their hovel and accusing his wife of hiding money; money which could and should, in his opinion, be best served by feeding his lust for wine.

After smashing a vase and passing out, Herringbone wakes up with his wife's black cat asleep on his chest. He screams at the feline, declaring his blind hate for the beast, before rising, casually abusing Annabelle and heading out for his nightly binge. Alas, with little to no money to his name, the barkeep soon tosses him out, sending Herringbone wandering the streets, begging strangers for coins and crying for "more wine". Things take a turn in his favor when he accidentally stumbles into an establishment patronized by aristocrats who are right in the middle of a gentlemanly wine tasting event. There, he is introduced to the preening Fortunato Luchresi, a man widely recognized as one of the world's most accomplished wine connoisseurs. This claim offends Herringbone who brags that Luchresi would be no watch to his palette in any such contest, calling the more refined drinker a coward for not facing him. This both piques the interest and ignites the ego of Luchresi and the pair agree to a sipping showdown.

The contest is a draw but Herringbone — who had been guzzling the poured samples — is hopelessly inebriated. Amused by his uncouth equal, Luchresi helps the man home where he is introduced to Annabelle. The chemistry between the pair is palpable and, as Herringbone blacks out in his chair, Annabelle and Luchresi find common ground in their mutual love of cats; as the drunken slob sleeps beside them, the pair fall into each other's arms.

Some weeks pass and we find Herringbone back at his favorite tavern, boasting to the barkeep that his wife no longer resists his drunken escapades and instead happily hands over her sewing earnings to him whenever he pleases. When the bartender asks how long this new dynamic has been going on, Herringbone looks into the ether, thinking, until it dawns on him that his wife's change of behavior has occurred at roughly the same time he had introduced her to Luchresi.

Confronting his wife about her infidelity, Annabelle admits that she and Luchresi are indeed in love and plan to marry, after which a visibly disturbed

Montresor (Peter Lorre) stares down the black beast that will be his undoing.

Locke (Vincent Price) turns his back on his daughter Lenora (Maggie Pierce).

Herringbone congratulates her as the screen fades to black. The next evening, Luchresi comes to pay the Herringbones a visit under the guise of friendship. Though Annabelle is nowhere to be found, Herringbone offers his "friend" a glass of fine amontillado wine and, as Luchresi drinks and questions the occasion for such an expensive drink, Herringbone reveals that they're there to celebrate Luchresi's death; the wine has been poisoned and Luchresi passes out.

Luchresi wakes to find himself chained to a wall in the basement, the body of the murdered Annabelle chained beside him while Herringbone toils away at bricking them both up into the wall. The pair now entombed, Herringbone goes back out into the night in search of drink and, after buying a round for his fellow merrymakers, mutters under his breath that his wife will no longer need her money "where she's gone". The barkeep raises an eyebrow as Herringbone passes out on the counter.

Back home later that night, Herringbone has a nightmare of his victims emerging from the wall and tearing off his head, tossing it back and forth as Annabelle's cat looks on. He's awakened by the appearance of two policemen who have arrived to search the home after the barkeep's concerned tip. As Herringbone wobbles down the stairs to show the police his cellar, he imagines the ghosts of Luchresi and Annebelle taunting him, followed by the screeching of a cat. The police hear the ghastly sound and determine that it's emitting from the newly constructed wall. As they smash the wall down and discover the dead lovers, all present are shocked to see a black cat — Annabelle's cat — perched on the head of his slain mistress. In his haste, Herringbone had sealed the feline up behind the wall alive, thus cementing his own doom.

"I had walled the black monster up within the tomb!" — Poe

TALES OF TERROR

"THE FACTS IN THE CASE OF M. VALDEMAR"

Terminally ill, wealthy businessman Ernest Valdemar puts his remaining days in the hands of a noted mesmerist, Mr. Carmichael. Carmichael's treatments prove effective in relieving Valdemar's perpetual pain and give the gentleman a peace of mind, much to the marvel and delight of his wife. However, his physician, Dr. Elliott James, is skeptical, thinking hypnotism to be a charlatan's trick, though he cannot deny the positive effect on his patient's sense of well-being. Valdemar informs Helene and Dr. James that he has given permission to Carmichael to put him in a trance at the point of death, to study the final moments of life and how long it takes for the spirit to leave the body. Helene and Dr. James are aghast and urge Valdemar to reconsider such macabre last act pursuits. Both Helene and the doctor mistrust Carmichael, who inexplicably asks for no payment for his services. Instead, Dr. James believes that Carmichael has his romantic sights set on Helene and has become obsessed with her.

Days later, as Valdemar lies on his deathbed, Carmichael, as agreed, hypnotizes the man, locking him deep within a somnambulant trance. Valdemar does indeed die and yet his spirit is trapped in a sort of limbo, his dissonant, tortured voice emitting from his atrophied lips, begging Carmichael to release him. Carmichael refuses, despite Dr. James and Helene begging him to do so. It seems Dr. James was correct in his assumptions of romantic fixation and Carmichael cruelly vows to never let Valdemar's soul free unless Helene marries him.

As nights turn into days and the seasons change, Valdemar remains in his undead state, eerily begging for release as his body begins to decay. Dr. James, at his wits end, pulls a gun on Carmichael who shows both the doctor and Helene that Valdemar himself wishes his wife to wed the hypnotist, the dead man's words clearly puppeteered by Carmichael's manipulations. Taking him aside, Helene tells Carmichael that she will marry him if he releases Valdemar immediately. His ego offended, Carmichael assaults Helene, an act which manages to animate the doomed Valdemar, his corpse rising from the bed and attacking the horrified Carmichael. When Dr. James breaks into the room, he whisks the traumatized Helene away, looking back briefly to see Carmichael dead on the floor, the oozing, putrefied shell of Valdemar draped over him. With Carmichael dead, Valdemar is finally at rest.

"And there was an oozing liquid putrescence...all that remained of Mr. Valdemar." — Poe

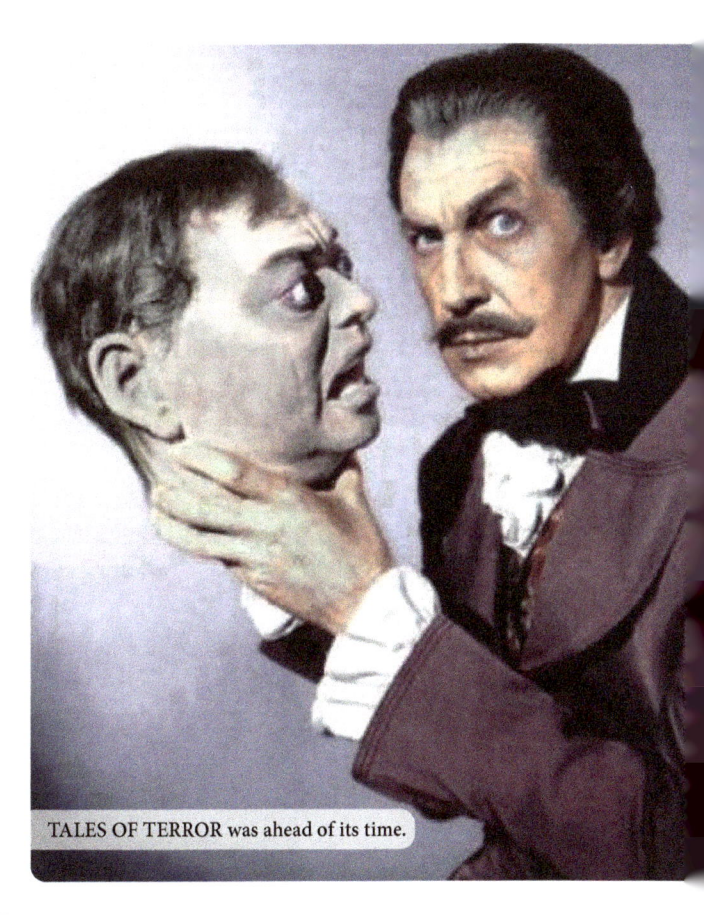

TALES OF TERROR was ahead of its time.

INTERVIEW: ROGER CORMAN ON TALES OF TERROR

ALEXANDER: There were but a handful of anthology genre films preceding TALES OF TERROR. Why did you decide to explore this format?

CORMAN: Well, when Dick Matheson and I began discussing what picture to do next, we both agreed that at this point in the cycle we were in fact repeating ourselves and the format of expanding the Poe stories — many of which were very, very short — had run its course. We came up with the idea of taking three Poe tales that actually — as is — lent themselves to the format of short filmmaking. So it made sense to us to do three short films connected by theme and author and that became TALES OF TERROR. It was an enjoyable shoot. We had a three week schedule as per usual, and that afforded us five days per story so it was fun to do.

ALEXANDER: TALES OF TERROR marks the first time in the cycle where the supernatural was not suggested but explicit.

CORMAN: That's true. In THE FALL OF THE HOUSE OF USHER and THE PIT AND THE PENDULUM, Dick and I were dealing in reality and again, working on those Freudian theories I was interested in surrounding the conscious and unconscious mind. The audience is occasionally fooled into thinking that they're experiencing something supernatural because of the ways in which the characters are tormented and interacting with the natural world. But you're right in that "Morella" specifically, is a supernatural story, with "The Facts in the Case of M. Valdemar" also toying with the supernatural, although there is also a scientific angle to it as well. "The Black Cat", however, is still in line with THE FALL OF THE HOUSE OF USHER and THE PIT AND THE PENDULUM's more internal, psychological leanings.

ALEXANDER: It's clear that humor was secretly woven into the previous Poe pictures, though the films themselves are not funny. But with TALES OF TERROR, you introduced a broad, fully realized undercurrent of comedy.

CORMAN: Yes. That was an intentional move to, again, make TALES OF TERROR feel different than its predecessors. Although, the comedy is actually only present in the second story — incidentally, my favorite story in the picture — "The Black Cat".

TALES OF TERROR

A clearer look at Ernest Valdemar's oozing final fate.

I initially was unsure about employing comedy to a story that was as deadly serious as this — with murder, spousal abuse, infidelity, people being buried alive — but it worked out well.

ALEXANDER: Is the comedic angle the reason why you cite "The Black Cat" as your favorite of the three tales?

CORMAN: Yes, but not just that. I would say the main reason why it was — and remains — my favorite of the stories is more due to the drinking sequence between Vincent Price and Peter Lorre. I loved it because, as Dick has said on numerous occasions, I usually stuck to the script, but in that case, I let the two of them improvise as they got drunker and drunker. Of course, they weren't really drunk, they were just acting, but what performances! It's just a wonderful scene and Peter and Vincent worked very, very well together and had so much fun. And so did I.

ALEXANDER: I've always enjoyed Joyce Jameson's work in that segment as well.

CORMAN: I liked Joyce very much; she was a very good dramatic actress and also very good with comedy; she could always bring a little note of humor that I liked, because it would lighten the mood before jumping right back into the macabre. She was very gifted in musical theater too and she got along very well with Peter and Vincent, working very well alongside them.

ALEXANDER: Her performance also adds an element of real pathos and tragedy to the film.

CORMAN: Yes, it does. I would say that her performance and timing is key to the piece's success; that balance between the absurdity of the piece and genuine concern for her character's situation.

After AIP put out the word, an army of kitties showed up for a shot at being "The Black Cat".

ALEXANDER: Did you have any issues corralling the cat on set?

CORMAN: I was initially concerned that we would. AIP launched a big publicity event where people would bring their black cats in to audition. But we went with a professional. We had a trainer who brought us a black cat and in pre-production, he showed us all the tricks the cat could do and how it could obey simple commands. On set however, it was a different story as the cat, for whatever reason, decided not to cooperate. However, the trainer had several back-up black cats with him and we were able to constantly rotate the cats to ensure the shots worked out as we wanted them to. So while there were some challenges, we made it all work well.

ALEXANDER: The driving through line in all three tales isn't just the story's author, but the presence of Vincent Price. Was there ever any debate as to Price playing the lead in the stories?

CORMAN: None whatsoever. Remember that the reason I didn't cast Vincent in THE PREMATURE BURIAL was simply because I had started that film independently of American International Pictures and Vincent was under contract with them for that sort of picture. So I went with Ray Milland, who again, I felt did a very fine job. But because TALES OF TERROR was an AIP picture right from the start, we had the opportunity to get Vincent without any issues.

ALEXANDER: "Morella" was originally intended to be the final picture in the film. Why did you change the order?

CORMAN: We noticed upon screening the picture in test screenings that something was off. "Morella" simply did not have the impact we needed for a closing segment so it we kept the comedy to the middle and started with "Morella" and finished with "The Facts in the Case of M. Valdemar" which lent the film a better rhythm and left a bigger impact on the audience.

ALEXANDER: At the end of "Morella", as with THE FALL OF THE HOUSE OF USHER, the house burns to the ground. Are those the same shots of the collapsing rafters edited into the finale?

CORMAN: Yes, they are. When we needed to show the house burning in THE FALL OF THE HOUSE OF USHER, we found an old barn that the farmer who owned it had planned to burn. So we paid him a few dollars to let us film it. I brought a small crew to the barn at night and we filmed it as it burned and collapsed and matched that footage to great effect with the sets for the climax. We shot so much footage of the burning barn for THE FALL OF THE HOUSE OF USHER that we re-used them for many other films, including this one. I became almost notorious for fire, in fact. When we shot THE MASQUE OF THE RED DEATH in England a couple of years later, the English crews had all been told about our tendency to use fire in our sets and that didn't sit well with them at all.

ALEXANDER: Can you elaborate on that?

CORMAN: Well, they were told — erroneously — that I had burned the set down of one of pictures we shot in the United States, either THE FALL OF THE HOUSE OF USHER or TALES OF TERROR, I'm unsure which. I didn't burn any set. I may have slightly singed the roof of one of them, but I'd never burned anything down. So they put all manner of restrictions on me, despite me explaining to them that we did not in fact burn anything down, outside of that barn.

ALEXANDER: "The Facts in the Case of M. Valdemar" benefits from the addition of the iconic Basil Rathbone as the villain. How was he to work with?

CORMAN: Basil Rathbone was a delight. An absolute professional. At this stage in his life he was much older and a little bit frail and he did admittedly have some trouble from time to time remembering his lines and had to take each scene point by point. I also had to soften my directorial approach somewhat with Basil, but I think he appreciated that sort of gentleness and the result was an excellent performance, I think. Vincent helped immeasurably as he and Basil knew each other and had worked together years previously, so their chemistry was set up before shooting.

ALEXANDER: You don't employ those "pure cinema" fantasy sequences in this story, but the climax, with Vincent melting to muck, definitely pushes its visuals in that direction.

CORMAN: Yes, it was the rare case of that style being applied to action that was set in reality as opposed to the unconscious mind. We had to prep a kind of wax — if I recall right it was wax, or maybe some other material. Regardless, we had to set the appliance up for the shot in stages to illustrate the fact that Vincent was indeed melting. Today, we could have easily done this with more sophisticated special effects or computer generated imaging, but then it was much more cumbersome. Using the distorted lenses added an element of horror but also obscured the effect enough that it became vague. That entire sequence, including when it transitions to the painting, worked pretty well, I think.

ANALYSIS

Appreciating TALES OF TERROR is an easy task; it's a joyous thing, full of color and drama and terror and pulp cinema bravado. But as with all anthology horror films, it's hard not to subjectively pick favorites. Even Roger himself cites "The Black Cat" as his own personal choice for the best entry of the three. Fair enough. "The Black Cat" is irresistible, with the trifecta of Price, Lorre and Jameson bouncing their energy off each other like jazz musicians. It's a loose, funny and utterly charming entertainment that also manages to be wickedly macabre and cruel, with a palpable tragedy at its core. It is, after all, a tale of vicious domestic abuse, with Jameson's performance broadly comic on one level, flustered and reactive to her husband's loutish behaviors. But Jameson's Annabelle is most certainly a battered wife, slave to a domineering, violent and hideous alcoholic who saps her soul and decimates her precarious finances. At one point, Jameson stares longingly into nothingness, defeated by her spouse and says to herself "he was so romantic…once". Jameson is SO good in the role that it's somewhat aggravating that Price and Lorre are generally the ones who garner all the accolades. Hers is a fully realized portrait of a woman slipping away, desperately trying to cling to something, anything decent around her. And when she encounters real empathy and kindness and love in the arms of the dashing Fortunato, we root for her, we WANT her to be saved and to rise above her situation. That she ends up humiliated yet again, murdered and strung-up and walled-up is gut wrenching. And we can credit Matheson's pen for so much of that humanity. In fact I'd argue that it's Matheson's scripts that offer the most depth in the Poe Cycle, the ones that function on multiple levels and always offer an emotional core and empathetic foundation for the terrors — and in the case of "The Black Cat", laughter — to come.

Similarly, "Morella" — though less showy than "The Black Cat" — is anchored by pathos. Here we have the story of a young girl whose simple act of being born sets forth a kind of karmic curse. There are no heroes in "Morella", if you consider the varying points of view. Lenora returns to her family home with a terminal illness, a capper to a life ripe with failure and misery. Her only aim is to confront her father and get closure for the inexplicable rejection she's received from him that's

TALES OF TERROR

Fortunato and Montressor toast their fates, united and doomed by their love of drink.

dictated the tapestry of pain she's had to endure. She's not heroic; rather she's broken, doomed by decisions made for her before she could walk. And her father is equally ruined; a man whose fractured heart has erected walls around it and who has learned, as a kind of defensive mechanism, to translate his pain into white-hot hatred, vitriol targeted squarely at the most vulnerable person within reach: his own child. And at the center of their shared trauma lies the body of Morella herself, a woman who died in childbirth, leaving her husband a widow and her daughter motherless. And yet even she has empowered herself with hate so intense it goes beyond the grave. Every character's existence is a miserable dead end.

If "Morella" is the weakest of the three stories, it's a direct result of its singular nihilism. It's short and vicious and mean and everyone dies in pain, save for the monstrous Morella herself, who returns from the dead to kill her child and her husband, and whose mummified corpse then incinerates with a smile upon her desiccated face. "Morella"'s shortcomings come only from its short length. Matheson is playing with so much complex misery here, a larger canvas to paint on would have made it a much more satisfying and involved experience, deepening the characters and making us identify more with their individual plights. It's no wonder Corman opted to alter the order of the tales; if audiences left the theater after enduring the bleak, moral void that is "Morella", they might very well have just strolled right into oncoming traffic.

Originally intended as the first story in the sequence, "The Facts in the Case of M. Valdemar" is indeed a much more effective closer and is a more fully realized story than "Morella"; certainly, its heroes and villains are more clearly defined and its emotional arc more accessible. Rathbone's malevolent mesmerist Carmichael oozes Svengali menace; Paget's tormented wife Helene is much more than just the token suffering female and Price is sweet and sympathetic as Valdemar, a man who literally falls under the spell of a sociopath and thus almost dooms his legacy, but whose decency and love transcends death itself. Even Frankham's faithful Dr. James gets moments of depth. And the entire tale is drawn together visually by that wonderful rotating piece of hypnotic psychedelia, one that keeps the eyeballs perpetually dazzled whenever Corman, Haller and Crosby place it in the frame.

Some have cited the lack of a coherent narrative wraparound device as a flaw in the film, but I personally love that the stories exist mostly on their own, connected only by Price's ominous narration, one that purports to be framing the movie as an expressive study in death. Hearing only Vincent's voice channeling the brooding lyricism of Poe is really all you need to make the wildly diverse stories flow together.

Further appreciation of TALES OF TERROR can be found in the long out of print pages of Eunice Sudak's paperback novelization of the film. The fact that the book doesn't just reprint Poe's tales, but asks Sudak to specifically create a troika of short stories based on a script that is in itself based on Poe is fascinating, and her versions expand just enough on what ended up on screen to add even more texture to the experience. The book

TALES OF TERROR

Lenora discovers the mummified body of her mother, Morella (Leona Gage)

restores the original order of tales, starting with "The Facts in the Case of M. Valdemar", which ends with a postscript detailing how Dr. James managed to cover up the unbelievable events of the story's climax, instead listing Carmichael's death as "drowning", which makes sense considering he was essentially smothered by the gelatinous goo that the zombified Valdemar had devolved into. In "The Black Cat", Sudak amplifies the dynamic between Annabelle and Montressor, hammering home the latter's booze-fueled vulgarity and making us feel even more empathy for his poor wife. We also get an interesting final sequence where the now incarcerated and waiting for the gallows Montressor feels perhaps a twinge of guilt for his crime and feverishly pens his confession. And in "Morella", we close on Poe himself scrawling the final lines quoted in the film, which takes some of the abruptness out of the story and instead neatly illustrates how the tale's themes of spectral vengeance, romantic obsession, necrophilia, family tragedy and madness encapsulate the very essence of Poe. Incidentally, the Dell Comics adaptation also maintains the original story flow of Matheson's screenplay.

THE RAVEN

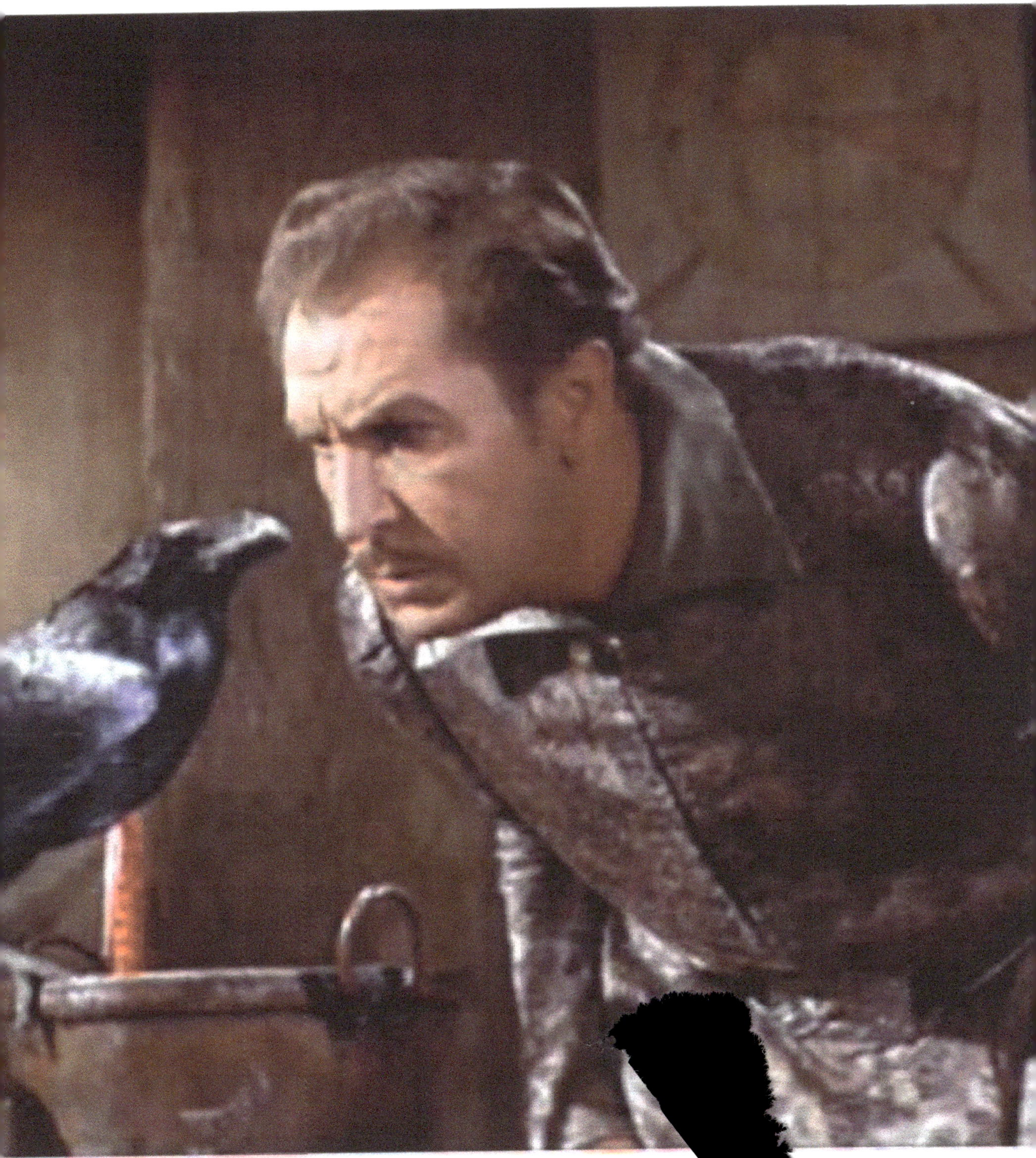

CORMAN/POE

CAST
Vincent Price as Dr. Erasmus Craven
Peter Lorre as Dr. Adolphus Bedlo
Boris Karloff as Dr. Scarabus
Hazel Court as Lenore Craven
Jack Nicholson as Rexford Bedlo
Olive Sturgess as Estelle Craven
Connie Wallace as The Maid
William Baskin as Grimes
Aaron Saxon as Gort

WRITTEN
Richard Matheson
Based on the poem "THE RAVEN"
by Edgar Allan Poe

CINEMATOGRAPHY
Floyd Crosby

EDITED
Ronald Sinclair

PRODUCTION DESIGN
Daniel Haller

SPECIAL EFFECTS
Pat Dinga

PRODUCED
Samuel Z. Arkoff, James H. Nicholson
& Roger Corman

DIRECTED
Roger Corman

SYNOPSIS

Magician Dr. Erasmus Craven sits in his study, his fingers gesturing in the air as he manifests a sketch of a large raven, all the while lamenting the passing of his dear departed lady love, Lenore. Though gone for over two years, Craven just cannot let her go, much to the dismay of his daughter who pleads with her father to forget about her stepmother and move on with his life. Later that night, while preparing for bed, Craven hears a rapping at what he first believes to be his chamber door, quickly surmising that the sound is coming from his window. There, on the other side of the glass, is the spitting image of the massive raven he was drawing earlier, pecking away at the glass, eager to come inside. Initially delighted, Craven allows the bird in but is shocked when the creature begins to speak. Craven soon learns that the bird is, in fact, the transformed wizard Dr. Bedlo, a second-rate sorcerer with a fragile ego who dared to challenge the powerful and feared magician Dr. Scarabus and got turned into a raven for his efforts. Bedlo is adamant that Craven should create a potion to turn him back into his rightful form and lists the vulgar ingredients needed for the task. Craven agrees and proceeds with brewing the remedy but ends up not making enough, only partially reverting Bedlo back into a man, leaving his arms a pair of black, feathered wings. Bedlo is outraged and demands Craven make more of the potion, despite being out of the key ingredient, the hair from a dead man. The hapless pair then venture down into the Craven family crypt to open the coffin of Craven's dead father, a once powerful wizard in his own right, and pluck a hair from his corpse. When they do so, the nearly mummified cadaver momentarily wakes up, grabbing his son's wrist and uttering a single word of warning: "Beware".

The second dose of antidote proves effective and Bedlo, now fully restored, toasts his liberator before revealing his intentions to go back and face Scarabus again, though Craven implores him not to do so. But when Bedlo recognizes a portrait of Lenore on the wall and tells Craven that he in fact saw her in the company of Scarabus that very night, Craven is shaken. The pair open Lenore's coffin and find her body inside. Bedlo is adamant that the woman he saw was Lenore, and if not, surely her double. Craven begins to suspect that Scarabus might have somehow imprisoned Lenore's spirit to enact some sort of vengeance against his family, as the elder sorcerer had long feuded with Craven's late father.

CORMAN/POE

Dr. Craven (Vincent Price) at the peak of his powers.

As the pair prepare for their journey to Scarabus' castle, Craven's coachman is suddenly seized by a spell and tries to kill Craven, Bedlo and Estelle with a battle axe. But Craven, using his own powerful magic, manages to wake him from his trance before he can finish his lethal task. Craven quickly surmises that it was Scarabus possessing his servant, a bid to prevent their journey.

Joined by Bedlo's hapless son Rexford, the quartet then set off to Scarabus' castle, with Rexford now driving the coach and trying to woo Estelle who is equally taken with the young man. However, Scarabus' will once more takes over and Rexford slips into mania, nearly driving their carriage off a cliff. However, the heroes soon arrive at Scarabus' fortress unscathed, and they apprehensively enter. They are greeted by a surprisingly warm and kindly Dr. Scarabus, who is gregarious and pleasant, charming the fair Estelle and flattering Craven, claiming any bad blood between himself and Craven's father was exaggerated and taken out of context. Craven accepts this, but still demands to see his dead wife, relating the tale that Bedlo had relayed to him. Scarabus denies all accusations of necromancy and instead summons his comely servant, implying that Bedlo in his drunken, irate state confused the younger woman with that of Craven's dead wife.

Satisfied with this and apologetic for their intrusion, Craven accepts Scarabus' invitation to join him for supper, though Bedlo is unbowed and demands a rematch with the elder sorcerer. The two engage in a duel, with Bedlo's feeble attempts to better Scarabus falling flat. When Bedlo attempts to conjure a storm,

THE RAVEN

a bolt of lightning zaps through the window and kills him, turning him into a puddle of raspberry jam.

With the four now mourning Bedlo's death, Scarabus urges them to stay the night as his guests to which they gratefully oblige. Later that night, Estelle is awoken by a noise and wanders the corridor where she encounters Rexford, who is suspicious of Scarabus and believes that his father's death was in fact intentionally caused by the sorcerer. Craven meanwhile is shocked to see Lenore appear at the window but when he investigates, she is gone.

We soon learn that Lenore is very much alive and had staged her death so that she could live with Scarabus as his lover. Scarabus does indeed want to obliterate the Craven dynasty and steal their magic; he had been using Bedlo to bait Erasmus's hook the entire time, sending him in his raven form to lure Craven to the castle with talk of Lenore. Bedlo then appears to Rexford, very much alive and reveals to his son that he is merely pretending to be loyal to Scarabus, part of his covert plot to kill him.

Now reunited Craven, Estelle, Bedlo and Rexford attempt to flee the castle but are stopped by Scarabus and imprisoned. Bound by ropes in their cells, Bedlo and Craven commiserate on their failures and their mutual enabling of Scarabus' evil when Lenore suddenly appears, taunting her former husband. Scarabus takes mercy on Bedlo and, instead of killing him, turns him back into the raven. Lenore and Scarabus place Estelle in a pillory, threatening to torture the girl to death unless Craven gives up his secrets. Meanwhile, Bedlo frees Craven's hands, allowing him to use his gesturing magic on Scarabus and the pair engage in a brief battle of sorcery. Scarabus calls for a reprieve and challenges Craven to a proper duel, this time to the death.

The wizards sit at opposing thrones and face off in a series of tricks, spells, illusions and attacks. Craven wins, defeating Scarabus as the castle burns. Lenore runs to Craven's side, begging him to take her, claiming that she was under the spell of Scarabus all along. Craven is unconvinced and turns away from her, accompanying Rexford, Estelle and the still-feathered Bedlo out of the burning building. In the rubble, Scarabus and Lenore dig out, very much alive, though Scarabus's powers have apparently ebbed.

Later that night, Craven relaxes with wine in his study while the still raven-cursed Bedlo begs Craven to turn him back into a human once more. Craven says he will consider it and Bedlo continues his raving and griping until Craven commands him to "shut your beak".

"Quoth the raven, nevermore" — Poe

Jack Nicholson as Rexford Bedlo in THE RAVEN.

INTERVIEW: ROGER CORMAN ON THE RAVEN

ALEXANDER: Following TALES OF TERROR, you further mined the comedic cocktail of Poe, Price and Lorre and added Boris Karloff and a young Jack Nicholson to the mix with THE RAVEN, which is fair to call an all-out spoof. Were you getting bored of the generally grim tone of the previous Poe pictures?

CORMAN: It wasn't so much boredom than the fact that, even by then and even after experimenting with the formula with an anthology film like TALES OF TERROR, I knew we were starting to really repeat ourselves; I was only getting bored by the formula, and we needed to keep trying to attempt something new with the pictures to keep them fresh. But it was Dick Matheson who really pushed for that. We had so much fun playing with comedy in "The Black Cat" that Dick suggested that we needed to go all the way and outright spoof ourselves, and I thought it was a great idea. It worked incredibly well and THE RAVEN was very successful.

ALEXANDER: I've always thought of your 1959 film A BUCKET OF BLOOD to be your first potent blend of broad spoof and horror, a sort of blueprint for the tone of THE RAVEN. In many ways there are elements of Poe in that story too, don't you think?

CORMAN: I think you're right. As I mentioned, I was always an admirer of Poe and there are certainly aspects of A BUCKET OF BLOOD that echo "The Tell-Tale Heart" and other Poe stories. Interestingly, that initial idea of combining horror and comedy in A BUCKET OF BLOOD came from one of my sneak previews. I've always been a strong believer in sneak previews, though I know many people don't like them because they're afraid of putting their movie before an audience. But with my horror pictures, I was a firm believer in doing them because you might get a laugh in the wrong place; your instincts about what was working might be wrong. So after a preview, you still have the opportunity to go back and fix the picture before release. So again, I was attending a sneak preview of one of my films and there was a scene where a character was walking down a hallway and suspense was building and building and there was a door at the end and the music and the sound were working fine. My idea was that the audience was torn between two thoughts: go to the end of the corridor and find out what's behind the door and at the same time, don't take another step, turn around and get out of there.

When the door was opened, something fell forward and the audience screamed and I thought

THE RAVEN

The unholy three (L-R): Boris Karloff, Peter Lorre and Vincent Price.

"I've done it, the scene works perfectly". But after they screamed, a number of people laughed, and I thought "What went wrong?" But nothing went wrong. They needed that laugh as part of their release. It's similar to being in a sexual situation, the same kind of tension builds and you come, that's the release. A BUCKET OF BLOOD was my answer to that and that led to (writer) Chuck Griffith and I to make THE LITTLE SHOP OF HORRORS, another even broader horror comedy, which I suppose also has some aspects of Poe as well in some respects.

ALEXANDER: It's been said of Karloff during his final decade, that even at his sickest he never missed a beat. How ill was Boris during the making of THE RAVEN?

CORMAN: I will say this: He was having difficulty walking. That was the only way his illness showed. When he was sitting or standing, there were no problems. I usually like to have lots of movement with my actors, so I had to work around this. As a matter of fact, now I'm remembering a scene in the film: Boris was at the top of a grand staircase and Jack Nicholson was at the bottom, and before we shot it,

Dr. Bedlo braces Estelle Craven (Olive Sturgess) while her stunned father sleeps soundly.

Boris came to me and said, "Roger, I really cannot walk down that staircase."

Now, understand, he could walk, just not that well. So I said, "Here's what we'll do, Boris. I'll photograph you at the top of the staircase, and you just take two or three steps down and I'll have somebody standing on each side of the camera so that if you slip, someone will catch you." He agreed to that. So I said, "The way we'll compose the scene is that I'll photograph you at the top of the stairs, then cut to Jack as he's looking up at you, then cut back to you as you start to walk down, then cut back to Jack as he's looking at you, then we'll take you to the bottom of the staircase and repeat the process as you're talking the last few steps." And the scene plays perfectly well; you cannot detect that Boris was having any difficulty whatsoever.

ALEXANDER: Did he have any trepidation about the moving platforms used during the climactic wizard battle?

CORMAN: Not really, in fact that scene was a joy to shoot and was rather ingeniously staged. Floyd Crosby and I came up with the idea of putting both Vincent and Boris mounted on their thrones on the ends of the crane while it moved around the set, with the camera then mounted in the middle of the crane pointing out to give the illusion that they were flying.

THE RAVEN

Vincent and Boris had no trouble or concerns about it and had great fun doing it, as did I, as did the entire crew and it was definitely a highlight of the shoot and the final picture.

ALEXANDER: Vincent once said that the scene where Scarabus throws the scarf at him — which turns into a snake — was somewhat unpleasant to shoot.

CORMAN: Well, I can't speak for Vincent, but I do remember that we had a snake wrangler on set who placed the snake around Vincent's neck and, if I recall, we had some difficulty getting the shot of the snake's head facing towards the camera. It all worked out, though it did take a bit longer than maybe Vincent would have liked!

ALEXANDER: Did Karloff get along with Vincent and Peter? Their chemistry in the film is perfection.

CORMAN: Generally speaking, yes, they did. There were some minor problems however, due in no small part to the varying styles of the actors.

ALEXANDER: Can you elaborate on that?

CORMAN: Well, all three were fine, fine actors. And again, they got along pretty well. The problems came from Peter [Lorre], who was excellent in the role but was prone to improvisation and he was excellent at doing this, drawing out more humor from the script and making the part his own. But you have to understand that Boris was a classically trained actor, who had worked extensively in England and when he prepared for a role, he went by the script as written and interpreted it in his performance. He came to the set prepared and knew all of his lines. But Peter was far less disciplined. He came to set with an understanding of the basic story and his character and used his lines as a guide. I think he actually had learned all his lines, he knew them, but he went in all sorts of improvisational directions with his performance. I don't quite think Boris understood how to react to this and it occasionally proved a challenge for me to make it all work, but it did and their dynamic in the picture is very, very funny.

ALEXANDER: How did Vincent fit into all this?

CORMAN: Vincent was ever the professional and also very charming and someone who could effortlessly make things work. He was an amalgam of both sensibilities. Like Boris, he was classically trained, and he stuck to the script, but he was very open to Peter's more playful approach, especially having recently worked with him in TALES OF TERROR. Most of Peter's improvisations happened during his scenes with Vincent alone, but I actually give great credit to Vincent for helping me draw Boris and Peter together during their scenes and be the sort of middleman to make their two opposing energies work so well.

Karloff's performance as the evil Dr. Scarabus stands as one his finest latter day turns.

CORMAN/POE

Somber portrait of THE RAVEN's central sorcerers.

ALEXANDER: How about the raven itself?

CORMAN: The raven? Oh, that was a nightmare! That damned bird caused me no end of trouble!

ALEXANDER: Did Matheson know that he was writing for Lorre and Karloff when he wrote the script?

CORMAN: Not initially. When we started, all we had was the poem by Poe, the understanding that Vincent would play the lead and the agreement that we were going to send-up the previous Poe films. Then he just invented this entire story. However, once Peter and Boris were cast, Dick finessed the script to reflect their personalities. And then Peter took his role a few steps further (laughs). I cast Jack Nicholson later, having worked with him several times before and having seen how well he could handle dark comedy from his performance in THE LITTLE SHOP OF HORRORS. He was cast as Peter's son and he did a fantastic job. He was young and understood "The Method" and he not only could keep up with Peter, the two of them developed their dynamic together. If you watch the picture, you will notice that Jack is constantly poking and pulling at Peter's clothes, tugging at his buttons and pulling stray threads and whatnot off of him, with Peter constantly slapping his hand away. The two of them had come up with the idea that Peter's character was deeply ashamed and annoyed by his son, while Jack idolized his father. It

THE RAVEN

added so much humor and personality to the picture and that was all credit to Jack and Peter.

ALEXANDER: It's not a Poe film, but it was built around the sets for THE RAVEN and is a fascinating sidebar to the Poe pictures. But who really directed 1963's THE TERROR?

CORMAN: Everybody and nobody [laughs]. Now, I've told this story so many times, but it's a good one, so I'll tell it again. THE TERROR was only made because it rained on a Sunday when I was going to play tennis. I had a week to go on THE RAVEN, and I was sitting in my house with nothing to do and the idea occurred to me that, hey, we had these really good sets, some of the best we'd ever had, and we were going to finish on Friday. I thought we could keep those sets up for a couple of days and I could shoot the beginning of another horror film, use my own money, close down and then, when I got some more money, shoot the rest of the picture.

So I called my friend Leo Gordon, a writer, and after a couple of drinks and dinner, we had the storyline worked out. I said, "Leo, what you gotta do this week is write 30 pages, and I'll shoot 15 pages a day for two days." I then asked Boris to stay over for two days before he went back to England, and he was happy to. Jack was there, and I explained that he'd play those two days with Boris, and told him, "You'll emerge as the leading man, and the whole rest of the picture will be on you." He said fine, only if his then-wife Sandra Knight could play the female lead, because they needed the money, and I agreed, as Sandy was beautiful and a good actress.

Now, what happened was that I couldn't shoot the rest of the picture because I'm signed with IA, the union, and I'm part of the Director's Guild, so I wasn't allowed to work. So let me think: I started the picture, Francis Ford Coppola shot some, Monte Hellman shot part of it, Jack Hill shot part of it and then at the end, with one day to go, Jack Nicholson said to me, "Roger, every idiot in town has worked on this movie, let me finish it!" The only problem was that every director varied the script, so the story doesn't hold together, but surprisingly, it did pretty well. It was a fun, interesting experiment and, for a quickie movie it ended up being the longest shoot of my career!

ALEXANDER: Do you think THE RAVEN's comedy still works today?

CORMAN: Yes, I think it does. I saw it screened with an audience not terribly long ago and they laughed just as hard as they did when we first released it. Unlike A BUCKET OF BLOOD, which I also saw a screening of not too long ago and noted that, while the audience did laugh in all the right spots, they didn't laugh as hard as they once did. I attribute that to many of the jokes that we were making then, about vegans and that sort of lifestyle, now being an acceptable component of mainstream society. Whereas when we made that picture, they were not at all part of the mainstream and therefore, much funnier to spoof.

ALEXANDER: Where do you place THE RAVEN in the cycle?

CORMAN: I don't really judge it the same way in which I would judge the other Poe pictures. First of all, it's based on a poem, just the basic idea of a raven appearing in a man's room. So what Dick and I came up with was wholly original. And it's a comedy, through and through. I place it outside the series in many ways but I certainly like it very much and I believe it has its own identity.

ANALYSIS

For their final Poe Cycle collaboration, Corman and Matheson opted to go out not with a bang, but a titter, literally and figuratively flipping the bird to the deliriously Gothic melodramatic morality plays that defined the series. THE RAVEN isn't the sort of side-glance, straight-faced gallows joke that was THE FALL OF THE HOUSE OF USHER and THE PIT AND THE PENDULUM, and it's not even really in line with TALES OF TERROR's "The Black Cat" segment either. No, for all its exuberant silliness, "The Black Cat" still had a grim, deadly serious story to tell and was macabre to its core. THE RAVEN, however, is a full-steam-ahead comedy of errors (one that Matheson would expand upon in his Jacques Tourner-directed 1964 AIP romp THE COMEDY OF TERRORS) that hasn't a serious bone in its body. Every streak of morbidity is punctured by a joke, every dose of depravity undone by a gag, every swell of atmosphere smothered by

The wicked Lenore (Hazel Court) and her dastardly lover.

THE RAVEN

Craven, Bedlo and Rexford stare suspiciously.

bug-eyed hysteria. And that's what makes it such a spectacular and singular entry in the canon.

Still, for all its irreverent lunacy and pitched-to-eleven performances, there is still a palpable sense of cruelty alive and well within THE RAVEN, even if it is played for laughs. Said cruelty comes — once more — in the form of a duplicitous and conniving woman. Price's Craven is — like Nicholas Medina in THE PIT AND THE PENDULUM — a cuckold, who wastes away pining for his wife and muse, who faked her own death not just to escape his affections, diving into the arms of his enemy, but to double back and literally destroy him. Court's Lenore is actually the most cold-blooded of the trio of femmes fatales she essayed for Corman, and she plays her role wonderfully straight, which makes the uneasy comedy milked out of her scenes with both Karloff and Price absolutely wonderful.

And regarding Karloff, despite his age and growing health issues, he is in top form here, veering brilliantly between warmly manipulative and sadistic, sometimes within the same scene. The actor excelled during this period embracing his "kindly old man" persona while disarming with just a single intense stare and colder dialogue delivery and his portrayal of the petty, narcissistic and merciless Scarabus is no exception.

THE RAVEN marks a turning point in the series. It's true that once a genre is spoofed, it's over and in many ways that's true of the Poe Cycle post-THE RAVEN. Corman never intended to make another one, instead turning his attentions to the more metaphysical and cosmic dread of H.P. Lovecraft in THE STRANGE CASE OF CHARLES DEXTER WARD, the movie that would be shoehorned into the series by AIP and baptized with the more Poe-centric title THE HAUNTED PALACE. That's a very, very different film in tone, in spirit, in style and intent. It's less romantic and more clinical, less Gothic and more overtly horrific and nihilistic. And after THE HAUNTED PALACE, when Corman crept back explicitly into Poe for the final two pictures, we see a new, darker and considerably more cynical sort of entertainment emerge.

THE HAUNTED PALACE

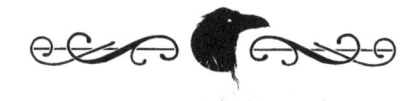

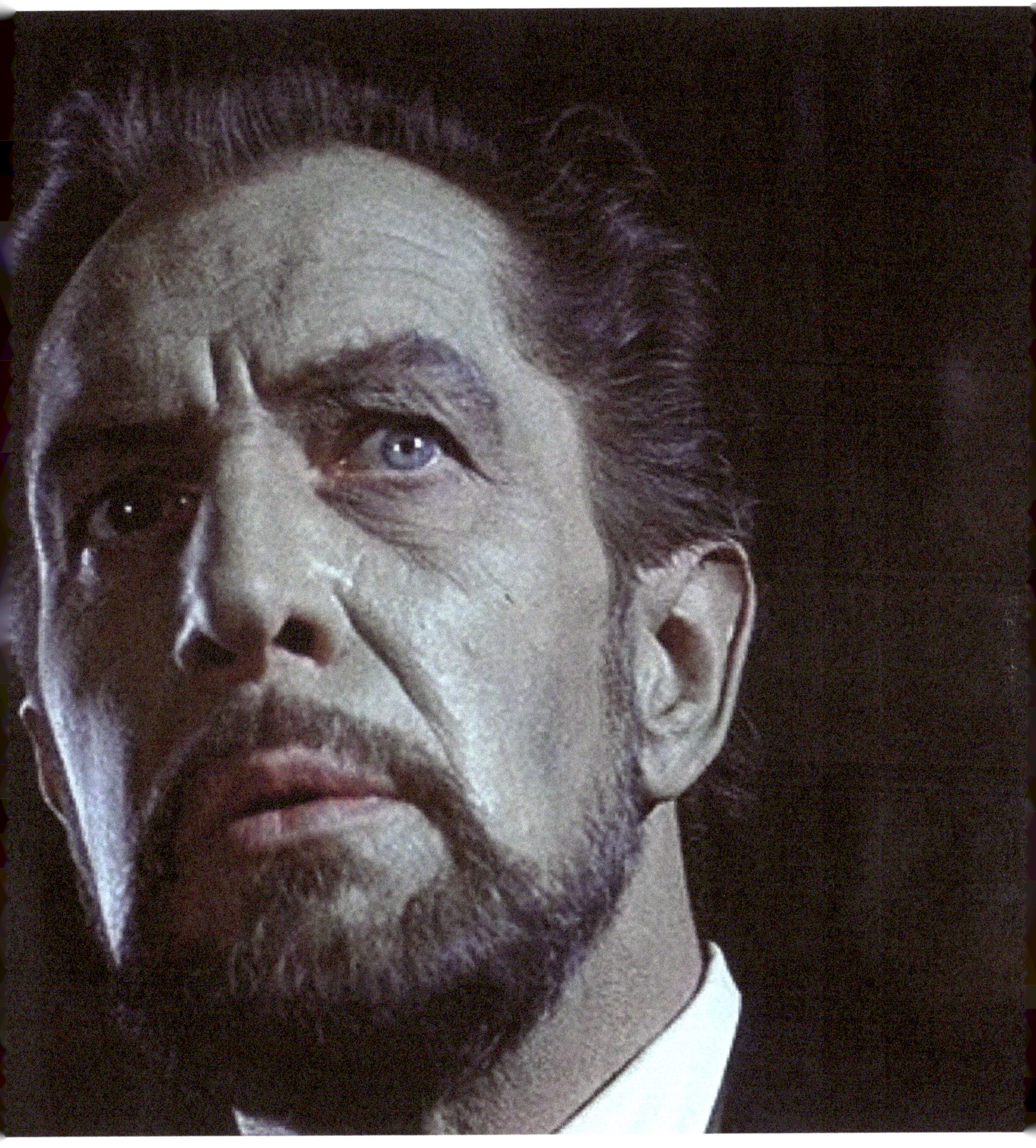

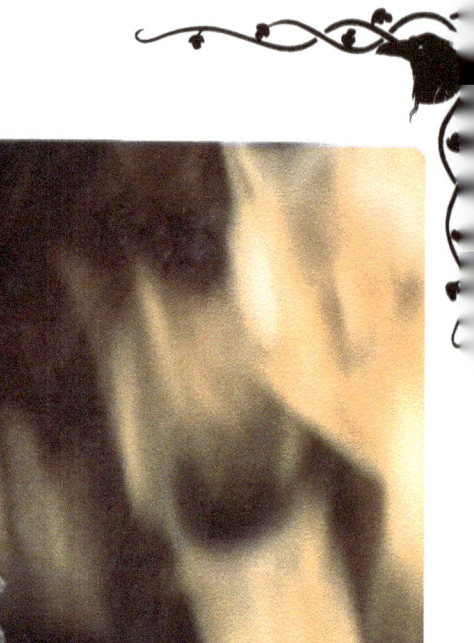

CORMAN/POE

Joseph Curwen (Vincent Price) curses his killers as the flames rise.

CAST
Vincent Price as Charles Dexter Ward / Joseph Curwen
Debra Paget as Ann Ward
Lon Chaney Jr. as Simon Orne
Frank Maxwell as Dr. Marinus Willet/Priam Willet
Leo Gordon as Edgar Weeden / Ezra Weeden
Elisha Cook Jr. as Benjamin West / Jacob West
Milton Parsons as Jabez Hutchinson
Guy Wilkerson as Gideon Leach
I. Stanford Jolley as Carmody
Harry Ellerbe as The Minister
Barboura Morris as Mrs. Weeden
Darlene Lucht as Miss Fitch
Bruno VeSota as Bruno

WRITTEN
Charles Beaumont & Francis Ford Coppola (uncredited)
Based on the story "THE STRANGE CASE OF CHARLES DEXTER WARD" by H.P. Lovecraft
Suggested by the poem "THE HAUNTED PALACE" by Edgar Allan Poe

MUSIC
Les Baxter

CINEMATOGRAPHY
Ronald Stein

EDITED
Ronald Sinclair

PRODUCTION DESIGN
Daniel Haller

SPECIAL EFFECTS
Ted Coodley

PRODUCED
Samuel Z. Arkoff, James H. Nicholson
Roger Corman & Ronald Sinclair

DIRECTED
Roger Corman

THE HAUNTED PALACE

SYNOPSIS

On a mist-drenched night in the village of Arkham, Ezra Weeden and some of the local men sit drinking at a pub, gazing out of the widow as a storm brews. They see a lone woman walking through the streets and, recognizing her, decide to follow. Their quest leads them to the front door of suspected warlock Joseph Curwen's monstrous estate, a place that they've long learned to fear.

The girl is taken by Curwen and his mistress to a deeply submerged basement lair and shackled above a gated pit. Reciting an arcane ritual, Curwen slowly opens the hole and, breaking from her trance, the girl peers down and screams. Weeden and the men push their way into Curwen's palace, dragging him outside into the woods and trying him to a pyre. Before the flames ignite, Curwen swears a blood curse on each and every man in the mob, a hex that will plague them for generations to come. Curwen is burned alive and dies screaming as lightning strikes and the rain begins to fall.

110 years later, a carriage rolls into the slightly modernized, still foggy, streets of Arkham. Emerging

CORMAN/POE

Charles Dexter Ward (Price) and wife Anne (Debra Paget) face the evil of Arkham.

from the carriage, Charles Dexter Ward and his wife Ann dismiss claims from their coachman that Arkham is an evil place and make their way through the streets to the tavern, The Burning Man, as the locals peer at them through broken windows. Ward tells the barkeep that he has inherited the Curwen mansion and Edgar Weeden, the ancestor of Ezra Wheaton, interrupts them, explaining that the house is cursed and that they should leave Arkham immediately. Charles and Ann shrug off the warnings and make their way to the palace on foot.

Along their way they see a little girl walking with her mother. The child's eye sockets are sealed shut and she limps along at her mother's side. Shaken but undeterred, they carry on, unbolting the front door's massive lock and entering the house. As they explore the astonishing interior, Charles spies the portrait of Curwen above the mantle, and both are shocked to see how closely the two resemble one another. Suddenly, the drawing room curtain pops and a heavyset man with gray skin appears and introduces himself as Simon, the caretaker. He apologizes for startling the couple and offers to take their luggage and set up their room. Ann tells her husband that she has no desire to stay inside the house overnight, but Charles, not wanting to offend Simon, insists they do.

Meanwhile, back in the village, Edgar Weeden wanders about his house, brooding, still visibly disturbed by Ward's arrival. He hears a growling from behind the wall and opens a latch, handing food to whatever lurks within. The creature grips Weeden's hand, clawing at him and he quickly burns it with the candle. He tells

THE HAUNTED PALACE

his wife the "thing" is especially aggravated because it knows who has come back to Arkham.

Back at the palace, Ward becomes more and more obsessed with his Great Grandfather's portrait and slowly begins to change; his gaze stiffening in a new sort of grim self-awareness while Simon, lurking in the shadows, stares on at this burgeoning transformation approvingly. The next morning, Ward, now fully possessed by the soul of Curwen, tells his wife that he plans to stay on indefinitely and that, if she objects, she should leave. Confused by her husband's icy demeanor, she vows to herself to stay with him for the time being to ensure that he is in no danger. Momentarily himself again, Charles and Ann go into the village in the evening to explore, only to find all the doors and windows of most of the homes and businesses shuttered. Suddenly the little blind girl appears, then more disfigured people come walking out from the shadows, their faces scarred, their eyes sealed over like the child's, their gaits troubled, and their bodies twisted. The people surround the couple menacingly and when the church bell tolls, their mission is interrupted and the spell breaks, sending them wandering back into the darkness of the alleys.

Later that evening, the couple dine with the local doctor, Dr. Marinus Willett, who explains that the misshapen people who bothered them were commissioned by Weeden in order to frighten Ward away. He says the town is haunted by fear, guilt and paranoia, all due to Curwen's evil reign. The villagers now believe that the generations of children born with mutations are a direct result of Curwen's sworn curse. He tells them it was thought that Curwen had possession of the Necronomicon, a book that would allow its owner to communicate with and summon the "elder gods" back to our dimension. Curwen's mad intent was to mate humans with these monsters and create a new master race. Though not superstitious by nature, the doctor believes Charles and Ann to be in danger and implores them to leave, to "Flee Arkham like you would a madman with a knife!"

Ward wanders the house alone later that night, disturbed, convinced that he hears the echoing sounds of his ancestor's execution a century prior. Simon appears again with Ward's coat, asking what his troubles are. Ward, seeing as Simon doesn't hear the noises he heard, suspects it was only the wind. Simon tells Ward to consult with the portrait of his Ancestor and, when Ward turns to gaze at the painting of Curwen, he becomes possessed once more. Simon explains that he is similarly possessed by his descendant, another Warlock, as is Jabez, the housekeeper. Their diabolical plan is to use Ann to resurrect Curwen's mistress Hester but first, Curwen vows to enact bloody vengeance upon the descendants

Now fully possessed by Curwen, Ward unearths a past love.

Curwen and Hester (Cathie Merchant) prepare Miss Fitch (Darlene Lucht) to meet the monster.

of those who sent him to death. Simon begs him to abandon such pointless plans and instead continue on with their mission to bring forth the dreaded gods Cthulu and Yog-Sothoth. Curwen dismisses him.

Later that night, Curwen, hiding behind the face of Ward, forces himself sexually on Ann, promising all manner of lurid pleasures. Ann wriggles from his grasp and runs off and Curwen goes out into the night to begin his rollout of revenge. First, he kills Edgar Weeden by opening the locked door that keeps the malformed thing in Weeden's wall at bay. This monstrosity, we learn, is in fact Weeden's son, one of the many suffering from Curwen's curse. Immediately after, he corners Peter Smith, descendent of Micah Smith, another of the men who executed Curwen, and burns him alive. Back at the palace, Curwen and his fellow revived Warlocks succeed in resurrecting Curwen's mistress Hester and Ann is offered up on the altar as a sacrifice to the "thing" in the pit. Meanwhile, the villagers, who have discovered Peter Smith's incinerated remains, light their torches and storm the palace, setting it ablaze; the flames reach the portrait of Curwen above the mantle, its destruction apparently breaking Curwen's hold on Charles. Dr. Willet appears and rescues Ann from the burning house, while Simon, Hester and Jabez flee, leaving Charles to die. Dr. Willet runs back into the house to pull Charles from the wreck just in time, dragging him outside where he is embraced by Ann. And yet, as Charles raises his head to look at his wife, there is a dark glimmer in his eye and a wicked smirk on his lips, making it clear that Curwen still has at least partial possession of Ward's soul.

"While, like a ghastly rapid river,
Through the pale door
A hideous throng rush out forever
And laugh — but smile no more" — Poe

INTERVIEW: ROGER CORMAN ON THE HAUNTED PALACE

ALEXANDER: We cite THE HAUNTED PALACE as a canon Poe picture, but, it's not a Poe film at all, rather it's an H.P. Lovecraft adaptation.

CORMAN: Yes, it is indeed based on a Lovecraft story, "The Case of Charles Dexter Ward," and that's exactly the title that I filmed it under and the one that is credited on screen. But AIP was so successful with the Poe name that they eventually stuck that on it. But because it was Lovecraft, it was much darker, more overt and less subtle, and much of that was because [screenwriter] Chuck Beaumont and I wanted a different approach to the general style of the Poe pictures I had been making.

ALEXANDER: Outside of the darker tone, how was adapting Lovecraft different from adapting Poe?

CORMAN: Aesthetically, the approaches were similar. Chuck and I had many discussions about how best to do this and what we chose to do was simply repeat some of the structural concepts that were applied to adapting the Poe pictures and that was to take the essence of the story and then draw in elements from some of Lovecraft's other stories to expand the main narrative and give it a bit more depth and make it more interesting and complex. Now, at some point after submitting his first draft, Chuck went on to work on another project, it could have been THE TWILIGHT ZONE, a series that both he and Dick Matheson were working on at the time. Or it might have been something else, I'm not sure. Regardless, I needed some more work done on the script and so I actually got Francis Ford Coppola — who was my assistant during this time and tended to do a bit of everything for me, including directing — to add some more detail and improve upon some of Chuck's dialogue. Of course, Francis didn't receive any on screen credit for the picture, but he contributed greatly to that script nevertheless.

ALEXANDER: Beaumont died far too young. What are some of your strongest memories of him?

CORMAN: Chuck was a really good guy and an interesting writer who — you're absolutely right — was cut off far too early before he could reach his full career potential. I first met him when I read a novel he wrote called THE INTRUDER, about racial integration in the American South, and I bought the novel and he wrote the screenplay and I was very pleased with it. And as you probably know, I made

Lon Chaney Jr. as Curwen's undead henchman Simon Orne.

the picture, critics liked it, it won a few festival awards and it was the first movie I made that lost money. Nevertheless, I was pleased with his work and I liked him and we collaborated several times after that.

ALEXANDER: You're always very diplomatic about the twists and turns of the film business, but how did you honestly feel about AIP shoehorning the film into the Poe series?

CORMAN: Well, first of all, for what it's worth, I think Lovecraft was a very good storyteller, but I do think Poe had a deeper and more complex way of writing. I will always prefer Poe. But to your question, I was actually okay with making the change the way AIP did, by grafting a line or two from Poe's writing onto what was a Lovecraft picture to justify the title. I suppose it was a bit of a cheat for Sam and Jim to do that, but I understood from a commercial standpoint why they did it. That's happened to me a few times with other studios; they change their minds somewhere along the line and you just have to roll with it. I suspect that AIP had it planned all along that they were going to release the film as a Poe picture, but that's fine, I wasn't angry then or now. If anything, the only real issue I had was that Poe's name was misspelled in the opening credit sequence!

ALEXANDER: Naturally, Floyd Crosby shot the movie, as he did all the US-based Poe films and yet the film is such a visual departure from the rest; desaturated and dirty.

CORMAN: Yes and that's exactly what the picture needed. Again, it didn't begin as a Poe picture and the story and tone is much bleaker than what we had previously created. Floyd used wide angle lenses to give a sense of atmosphere to the sets and we opted for a much more starkly lit picture because I felt that, although supernatural, Lovecraft was much more realistic in that what was happening was happening in the real world, as opposed to the more psychological, internal aspects of Poe.

ALEXANDER: Did you stick to the same two-week schedule with THE HAUNTED PALACE as you did with the other Poe films?

THE HAUNTED PALACE

CORMAN: Yes, we had a 15-day schedule — like we did on all the pictures — which was barely enough time to make what was a considerably complex film. But, like always, it didn't allot us very much time to have terribly involved discussions about character or motivation with the actors. Thankfully, by this point I had a kind of system worked out with Vincent where we would discuss the character before we went to camera so that when we were shooting, we understood each other. Though admittedly, having Vincent playing two characters in the film was a bit more challenging.

ALEXANDER: However, he also played two characters in THE PIT AND THE PENDULUM.

CORMAN: While in a sense that is true, in THE PIT AND THE PENDULUM he was actually mostly playing a single character who, in his psychosis, thinks he's his own father. Well, except in the flashback sequence, of course, where he is actually meant to be his father. But in THE HAUNTED PALACE, Vincent's duality is much more pronounced; he literally is two different individuals and I think his performance is much more complex, with his performance as Charles Dexter Ward being very subtle and vulnerable, the opposite to the more malevolent persona of Joseph Curwen.

ALEXANDER: Ronald Stein's theme for THE HAUNTED PALACE is a huge part of its power. It gets stuck in your head, long after the movie has finished. Did you work closely with your composers on these pictures?

CORMAN: No I didn't work closely with my composers very much. I figured, I'm not a musician, I can't tell them how to write music. What I would do, I would tell the composers what mood it was I was trying to capture, what would be the theme of the picture running all the way through and the changing of those moods during key scenes. Having explained that to the composers, I stepped totally away from the process until the score was delivered. I do believe Ronny's score for THE HAUNTED PALACE might be his best work, or at least it's the one that most people ask me about.

ALEXANDER: Lon Chaney Jr.'s first appearance coming out of the shadows is alarming; one of those jolting appearances you usually reserved for Vincent.

CORMAN: Yes, and it got quite a scream when we screened it!

The eyes of Joseph Curwen leer forth from a portrait hanging in THE HAUNTED PALACE.

ALEXANDER: Did you always attend the screenings of your films?

CORMAN: Yes, I would always make it a point to see the films with an audience, to gauge what worked and maybe what didn't.

ALEXANDER: Chaney's facial make-up in the film is a ghostly grayish green, which clearly illustrates he's not a man to be trusted!

CORMAN: Yes, and it works because THE HAUNTED PALACE is a supernatural horror film, as opposed to most of the Poe films which were not. That sickly skin tone is also evident on Charles Dexter Ward when he too becomes possessed by his evil ancestor.

ALEXANDER: Was Chaney easy to work with?

CORMAN: Lon was a very kind man, very friendly and professional and, despite his hulking size, very gentle. I enjoyed working with him and I think we made a good choice. At one point, it was suggested I hire Boris Karloff for the role of Simon Orne but he wasn't the right fit and Boris was far too frail at this point. Lon had the right quality of menace, and he was also enough of a name that it helped sell the picture.

ALEXANDER: There's a lot of eerie special effects make-up employed in THE HAUNTED PALACE as well, the work of artist Ted Coodley. What are your memories of Ted?

CORMAN: I had worked with Ted several times previously in earlier films like I, MOBSTER and he had also done exceptional work on some of the other Poe pictures. I really liked his work in THE HAUNTED PALACE, especially what he did with the mutated townspeople, with their facial disfigurements, which were very effective. Ted knew how to deliver quality makeups within the tight timeframes we had to shoot these pictures.

ALEXANDER: Daniel Haller's sets here are sprawling. Truly astonishing, especially that monstrous basement…

THE HAUNTED PALACE

CORMAN: As usual, we really didn't have much money on any of these pictures. At every studio, there's what they call the "scene dock". When a picture's finished and the set is torn down, they put a number of flats on the scene dock. So Danny, starting with the first picture, would go down to the scene dock and pull out a number of flats and had new flats made to build on them. And then those pieces would go back to the scene dock and for the next picture, he would do that again, taking the flats out from the first picture and building onto them. So by the time we got to THE HAUNTED PALACE, we had a considerable wealth of sets left over so it looked much bigger because it really was!

ALEXANDER: Was Haller particularly technical about his craft? Or did he just design by instinct?

CORMAN: The latter, I would say. In the early days, we'd go for lunch to discuss the picture we were making and Danny would just sketch out what he imagined on a napkin and we would agree or disagree with his ideas. He would walk onto the set with chalk and just sort of mark on the ground or walls where he thought the sets should be placed, as opposed to the way it was done in the big studios where you had a team of artists and draftsmen meticulously planning everything, which I believe is a waste of time. The set is constantly changing anyway, depending on the shot or the lens so I believe Danny's way was the right way!

ALEXANDER: How do you feel about THE HAUNTED PALACE today, in the context of the series or otherwise?

CORMAN: I always liked the picture, and it did very well commercially and critically. Because it's not really a Poe film, I suppose it's a bit of an anomaly in the series, but I still feel it has the essence of the other films. It was me attempting again to do something different, in this case a different writer's work entirely. But with the presence of Vincent and so many of my regular crew working on the picture I'm fine with it being considered a part of the series, if a somewhat strange part.

The Wards are powerless against Curwen's evil influence.

ANALYSIS

THE HAUNTED PALACE is the most nihilistic and oppressive of all the Poe pictures. It's sort of a miserable experience really; a dark, bleak, cruel and ugly supernatural melodrama with nary a ray of sunshine or moment of mirth to be found and no particularly virtuous hero to root for. Of course, much of this new, miserable sheen that's washed over the picture comes from the source material itself, of which the film is a relatively faithful adaptation, and the more elemental style of its author. Lovecraft's work was the antithesis of Poe's florid romanticism, mostly devoid of his perpetual sense of melancholy and that sort of subjective, interior monologue psychological ambiguity that Poe — and Corman's previous Gothic works — traded in. On that note, THE HAUNTED PALACE is almost pornographically direct. Some of this also has to do with Beaumont's script, which unlike Matheson's work, saps any and all mystery from the story almost immediately. That was always the big difference between the two friends and colleagues, and that's evident in their contributions to THE TWILIGHT ZONE as well. Beaumont was always more interested in the mechanics of plot than he was creating anything particularly immersive or enigmatic. With THE HAUNTED PALACE, the audience knows Joseph Curwen is absolutely wicked from the get go, and we know that Ward will in turn follow in his ancestors' diabolical footsteps. It's never a matter of will he succumb to Curwen's evil influence, it's a matter of when and then reveling in the unapologetically evil nature of his deeds. Under Matheson's guidance, THE HAUNTED PALACE would have an element of surprise, a reveal, a twist of some sort. There's almost none of this here. Because of this, I have always felt THE HAUNTED PALACE to be the least interesting of the cycle, though admittedly comparing it to Matheson's Poe films or even Beaumont's own contributions to the cycle is unfair because, again, THE HAUNTED PALACE is not a Poe film at all.

Despite its shortcomings, THE HAUNTED PALACE is still a marvelously horrific entertainment and there are endless elements to savor here. Stein's thundering score and majestic main theme is unforgettable, though admittedly tends to be overused, harming some quieter, suspenseful moments that would have benefitted from a gentler musical passage. Haller's sets are jaw-dropping (when are they not?) and his cavernous basement, with its cellar alter and demonic portal, feel

THE HAUNTED PALACE

absolutely surreal, less psychedelic than the chamber found in THE PIT AND THE PENDULUM and more like a sort of alternate dimension existing within the palace itself (Haller would later go on to direct 1969's Lovecraft adaptation THE DUNWICH HORROR for AIP and go full bore psychedelic with it; it's a fantastic little picture indeed). In terms of atmosphere, Corman is clearly pushing things as far as he can here, moving his players endlessly through those "vaginal" corridors of his and up and down monolithic staircases while turning the streets of Arkham into eerie, fog-drenched nightmare realms. I think THE HAUNTED PALACE might also bear the influence of the Italian Gothics that began sprouting up during this period, most of which were inspired in part by those first two Corman/Poe chillers and, to a lesser extent, the pulpier films coming from the Hammer Studios factory (later Hammer films like VAMPIRE CIRCUS also bear the mark of being, in turn, influenced by THE HAUNTED PALACE). The film indeed feels very much tonally like Mario Bava's BLACK SUNDAY or "The Wurdulak" segment in Bava's BLACK SABBATH (both incidentally distributed stateside by AIP), thoughCorman's direction is far more practical and less fluid than Bava's.

The cast is universally excellent too, and Price is clearly relishing flitting between two sides of the same genetic coin, often within the confines of a single scene, and it's great to see old pros like Chaney and Elisha Cook Jr. appear in a Corman picture, though never sharing a scene. And though it is somewhat distracting to see Cook, Leo Gordon and others essay the parts of their own ancestors, the gimmick adds a sort of "karmic curse" weirdness to the proceedings that really works.

But again, make no mistake, this is not a true Poe film. It is a Lovecraft picture and a good one (and, the first one, incidentally). Seeing the traditional series Poe quote grafted onto the finale of the film is as jarring as it was when AIP later tried to link Michael Reeves' 1968 historical horror masterpiece WITCHFINDER GENERAL (also starring Price in one of his most chilling and disciplined performances) by popping in some Price narration, a Poe quote and uselessly re-christening it THE CONQUEROR WORM, after the Poe poem. In our conversations about THE HAUNTED PALACE, Corman was his usual diplomatic self when talking about AIP's shenanigans, as he always has been publicly, but I still believe that, privately, it must have been a point of contention. While time and tide have accepted and embraced THE HAUNTED PALACE as a sort of hybrid Poe picture, Corman was forever trying to do new things and defy expectations and the association with that series must have been beyond aggravating for all creatively involved.

In both of his THE HAUNTED PALACE roles, Vincent Price mesmerizes.

THE MASQUE OF THE RED DEATH

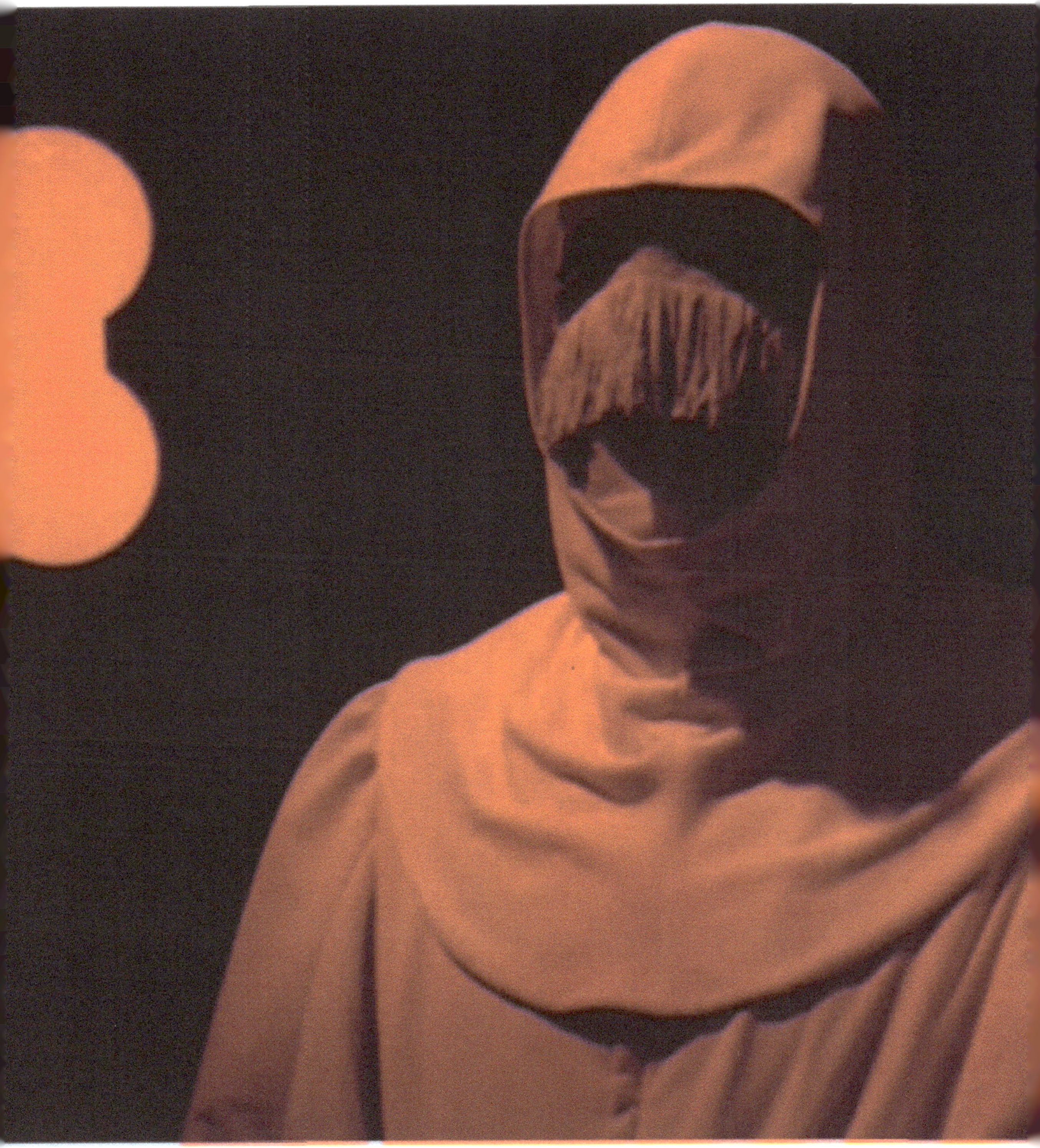

CORMAN/POE

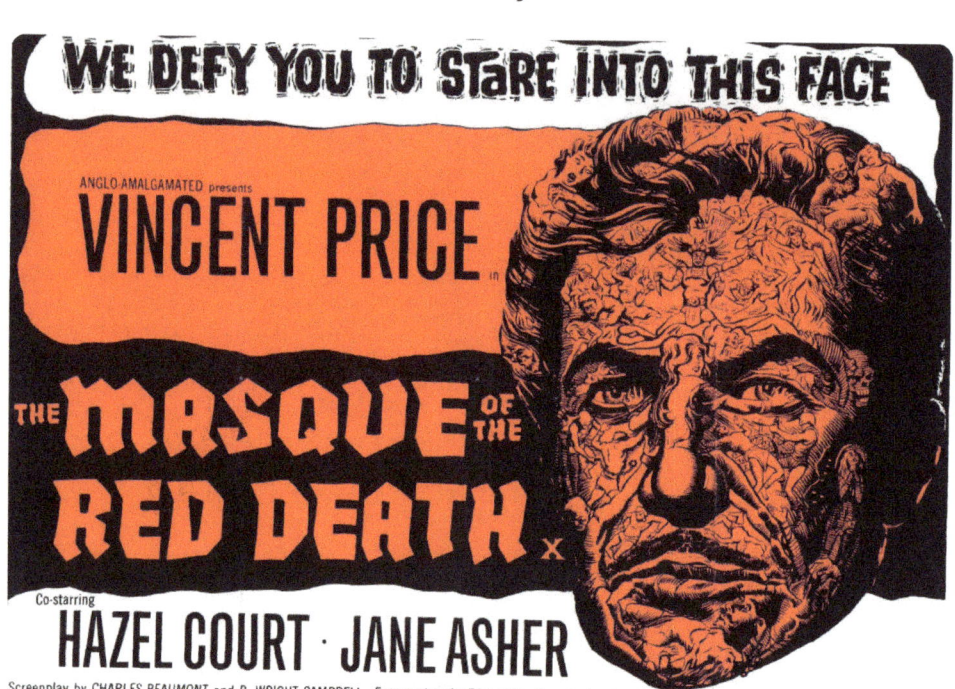

WE DEFY YOU TO STARE INTO THIS FACE

ANGLO-AMALGAMATED presents
VINCENT PRICE in
THE MASQUE OF THE RED DEATH
Co-starring **HAZEL COURT · JANE ASHER**

Screenplay by CHARLES BEAUMONT and R. WRIGHT CAMPBELL From a story by Edgar Allan Poe Produced by GEORGE WILLOUGHBY Directed by ROGER CORMAN
Print by TECHNICOLOR   An ANGLO-AMALGAMATED PRODUCTION   RELEASED THROUGH WARNER-PATHE

CAST

Vincent Price as Prince Prospero
Hazel Court as Juliana
Jane Asher as Francesca
Patrick Magee as Alfredo
David Weston as Gino
Nigel Green as Ludovico
Paul Whitsun-Jones as Scarlatti
Skip Martin as Hop Toad
Gaye Brown as Senora Escobar
Verina Greenlaw as Esmerelda
Brian Hewlett as Senor Lampredi
Doreen Dawn as Anna-Marie
Sarah Brackett as The Grandmother

WRITTEN
Charles Beaumont & R. Wright Campbell
BASED ON THE STORY "THE MASQUE OF THE RED DEATH" by Edgar Allan Poe

MUSIC
David Lee

CINEMATOGRAPHY
Floyd Crosby

EDITED
Nicolas Roeg

PRODUCTION DESIGN
Daniel Haller

SPECIAL EFFECTS
George Blackwell

PRODUCED
Roger Corman & George Willoughby

DIRECTED
Roger Corman

THE MASQUE OF THE RED DEATH

SYNOPSIS

In a remote medieval Italian wilderness, a hooded figure sits shuffling a deck of Tarot cards. When an elderly woman walks near the man, he hands her a single white rose that with a touch of his hand becomes spattered with drops of blood. The figure tells the woman to bring this "sign" back to her village.

Sometime later, the wicked Prince Prospero rides into the village with his guards to bully and intimidate his subjects, basking in the control he has over them. When he hears the story of the old woman and her encounter with the mysterious stranger, he visits the woman's hovel only to find her blistered and bloody and deep in the thralls of a plague. The prince fearfully exits the woman's home, citing the disease to be "the red death" and orders the entire village burned to the ground, taking three peasants with him as prisoners: Ludovico, Gino and Ludovico's beautiful daughter (and Gino's lover) Francesca.

Prospero returns to his castle and immediately sends word to his wealthy, aristocratic friends and the local nobility, inviting them to a grand masque, omitting the fact that a virus is spreading across the land. Locking Gino and Ludovico in the dungeon, Prospero orders his mistress Juliana to bathe and dress Francesca, a request that the jealous Juliana reluctantly obliges. Juliana briefs Francesca in the ways of the court and the nature of her connection to Prospero, which goes beyond sex; she and the prince are Satanists, something that further revolts the pious, virtuous Francesca.

Prospero arrives to escort his new feminine plaything to greet his guests, an assortment of entitled, arrogant Lords and Ladies who, once assembled are then informed by Prospero of the Red Death's presence. While initially horrified by the news, Prospero assures them that he and only he will offer them salvation and sanctuary if they in turn obey his every whim.

Prospero takes Francesca on a tour of the castle and the pair discuss their dueling faiths, the nature of man and morality, all the while exploring a series of monochromatic rooms. Later in the ballroom, Prospero forces his guests to engage in a series of humiliating games, while Prospero's dwarf, the articulate and wise Hop Toad and his equally diminutive ballerina lover perform for the court. That night, a jealous Juliana sneaks into Francesca's chambers, promising to help her escape the castle

CORMAN/POE

The Man in Red (John Westbrook) and the child he has chosen to spare.

and giving her the dungeon keys that will also liberate Gino and Ludovico.

Francesca, Gino and Ludovico follow Juliana's instructions and flee, looking for the palace guard that Juliana had paid to aid their exit. Instead, they are surprised by Prospero, who was well aware of their plan all along. Using the logic of Francesca's faith against her, Prospero cites that her father and lover have "sinned" and that evening he drags them in front of the court to engage in yet another game. The prince places a series of daggers on the banquet table, one of them laced with poison, and orders the men to cut themselves. However, Ludovico refuses, lunging at Prospero with one of the daggers and is quickly killed by a guard. As Francesca screams, Prospero then orders Gino killed as well, though at Francesca's pleading, he instead simply exiles the young man, allowing him to take his chances against the Red Death.

Threatened by Francesca's presence and desperate to win Prospero's favor, Juliana tells the prince that she has decided to submit to the final ritual and marry herself to Satan. Come nightfall, she ventures into the black room, drinking from an ornate ceremonial goblet while engaging in a series of hallucinatory rituals. However, upon completion, Juliana is attacked by Prospero's falcon, the bird pecking and clawing at her until she dies of her wounds. Prospero enters and smilingly approves of his former lover's grisly death, assuaged in the knowledge that she has given herself to Satan.

Meanwhile, wandering in the woods, Gino meets the red-cloaked figure who draws a card from the tarot

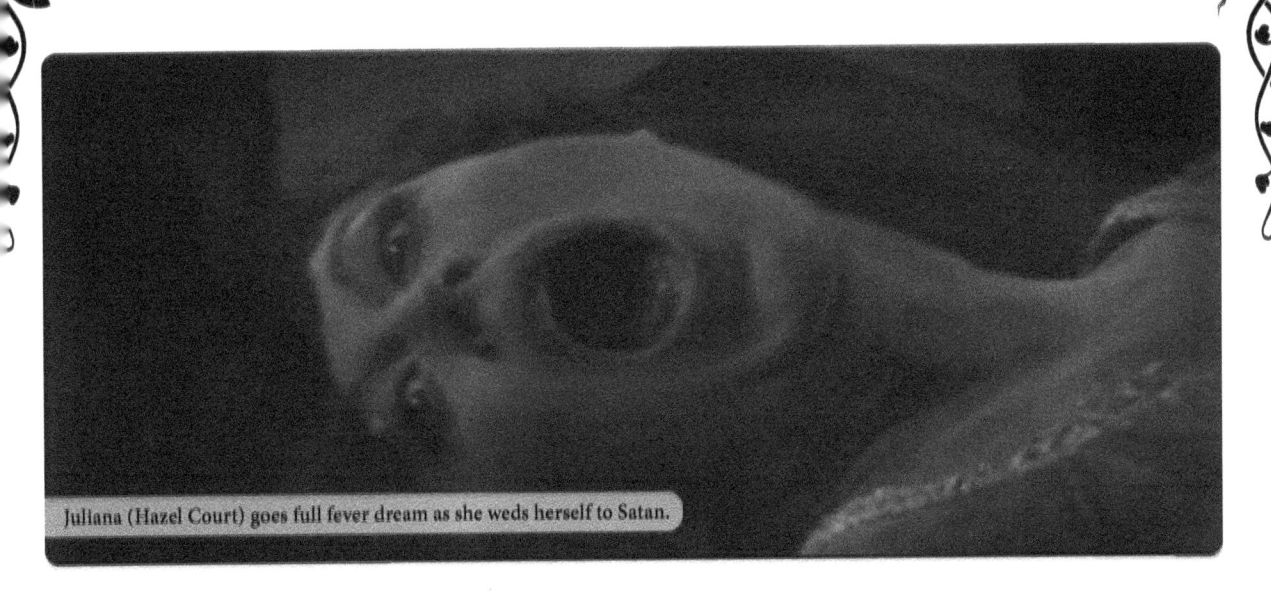

THE MASQUE OF THE RED DEATH

Juliana (Hazel Court) goes full fever dream as she weds herself to Satan.

deck, urging him to have faith. As a ragtag band of villagers pass him, intent on going to the castle to beg Prospero for sanctuary, Gino pleads with them not to go. They continue their journey regardless, and are promptly shot down by Prospero's crossbows, the wicked prince sparing only a little girl.

Back in the castle, Hop Toad reflects upon the previous day's events, wherein the sneering Alfredo had hit his lover Esmerelda when she refused his advances. He endears himself to Alfredo, encouraging him to make a bold presence at Prospero's impending masque ball, in which the guests are forbidden to wear red. Hop Toad suggests Alfredo dress-up in a moldering gorilla costume found in one of the castle's closets. Alfredo likes the idea, and, on the night of the soirée, the pair appear, Alfredo in the gorilla outfit and Hop Toad playing his whip-wielding trainer. Seeing a window to enact his revenge, Hop Toad ties Alfredo to a lowered chandelier, soaks him in wine and sets him ablaze, raising the screaming nobleman above the crowd. As Alfredo dies screaming, Prospero, first repelled then amused by the grim spectacle, tells his guards to find the fleeing Hop Toad and reward him for his "grand jest".

Gino returns to the castle to rescue Francesca and meets the red hooded figure, who tells him to stay outside and be patient. As the guests inside drink and make merry, Prospero guides the defeated Francesca through the crowds when he suddenly spots the red-hooded man. Outraged by what he thinks is one of his guests breaking his rule of wearing red to the ball, Prospero and Francesca follow the figure, the prince ordering the red-cloaked man to stop. They follow him into the black room and Prospero demands

Despite her unholy vows, Juliana dies screaming.

The evil Prince Prospero (Vincent Price) woos the pious Francesca (Jane Asher). Or is it the other way around?

to see the hooded wraith's face. When the specter refuses, Prospero comes to the conclusion that the figure is in fact an emissary of Satan, come to claim him and crown him as one of Hell's elites. With a wave of his hand, the figure infects the party — save for Prospero and Francesca — with the Red Death. Mesmerized and in a kind of somnambulistic trance, they begin to slowly, rhythmically dance. Prospero asks the figure to spare Francesca and the prince shares a tender moment with the young woman, and they kiss. Before he sends her on her way, he promises to meet her outside after his presumed Satanic ceremony is complete. However, the figure balks at Prospero referring to him as "excellency" and states that he indeed serves no master, angelic, satanic or otherwise. The figure is unmasked to reveal the blood dripping face of Prospero, the Prince's plague-ridden mirror image. Recoiling in horror, Prospero is groped by the infected, dancing guests before stumbling back into the black room, where the Man in Red informs him that his "soul has been dead for a long time". Prospero dies, his face melting into a red, bloody mess.

Later that night, deep in the woods, the Man in Red sits with the little girl whose family was murdered by Prospero's men. They play with a Tarot deck, laughingly revealing cards and enjoying each other's company. Suddenly, other color-coded cloaked figures emerge from the forest and discuss their respective body counts. The Man in Red tells his brethren of the people that perished as he passed, revealing that only the little girl, Hop Toad, Esmerelda, Gino, Francesca and a solitary old man from the village were spared. The Man in Red then stands and joins the rest of the plagues and they wander off into the night.

"And darkness and decay and the Red Death held illimitable dominion over all" — Poe

INTERVIEW: ROGER CORMAN ON THE MASQUE OF THE RED DEATH

ALEXANDER: Why did you decide to move production from Hollywood and instead mount THE MASQUE OF THE RED DEATH in England?

CORMAN: That was simply a matter of economics. There was an English tax law active at the time that refunded a percentage of the distribution costs of the film to the production as long as the picture itself was shot in England and employed a primarily British cast and crew. So Anglo-Amalgamated, who had great success distributing the previous Poe pictures in England, convinced us to shoot in England and basically, the British government subsidized the making of THE MASQUE OF THE RED DEATH. But as all things happen as they should, MASQUE was — in my estimation — a much better film for its employ of those performers, although the crew, while first rate, moved a little bit slower than the American crews I had worked with. Much slower than I would have liked, though really, that gave us more time — the shoot was about five weeks, I think — to really develop the look of the picture. We had many sets left over from the epic British period dramas BECKET and A MAN FOR ALL SEASONS available to us and Danny Haller built our sets out of the shells of those incredible sets. I'd say that without a doubt, MASQUE is the most grandiose of all the Poe pictures.

ALEXANDER: What's interesting about the Poe films is that although, by this point, they often explored the supernatural, there is nary any talk of religion in any of them. But in THE MASQUE OF THE RED DEATH, the dialogue is permeated with it. Were you trying to say anything particular about your own faith?

CORMAN: I would actually say I am an agnostic, though yes, I am very much interested in all religions and was happy to explore some of those questions here. A lot of that dialogue in THE MASQUE OF THE RED DEATH was deliberately put in by me, working with Chuck and co-writer Bob Campbell, and the way I wanted to interpret it had a quasi-religious feeling.

ALEXANDER: And you went so far as to make Prospero, not only a bastard, but full-blown Satanist!

CORMAN: Well, yes but I see it as more Prospero using Satan to actively reject God, and thereby rejecting natural law. By convincing himself God doesn't exist or that he's above God, he gives himself free reign to do as he pleases.

After laying waste to the land, The Man in Red reunites with his fellow plagues.

ALEXANDER: And the plague just gives him license to play God while walled in his kingdom.

CORMAN: Yes, exactly.

ALEXANDER: Were you surprised that the Catholic Legion of Decency condemned the film as "morally objectionable" in the U.S.?

CORMAN: As somewhat of a lapsed Catholic myself, I can't say I was particularly surprised, but we did make some small changes, mostly dialogue, to the picture for its domestic release. They read much of the film wrong, but we worked with them to find a reluctantly amicable solution.

ALEXANDER: What was the biggest difference between using cinematographer-turned-director Nicolas Roeg to shoot THE MASQUE OF THE RED DEATH, as opposed to Floyd Crosby?

CORMAN: They were both brilliant cameramen, though Floyd had to work faster with our shorter schedules in the U.S., but Nick had more time to light the set. I hired him because he was young — as was I — and he had a kind of vision and style and I felt that he could give me exactly the sort of rich, textured, saturated look I wanted for this film, one that would set it apart from the other films. Something dark and ominous when needed and then bright and garish in other sequences.

ALEXANDER: THE MASQUE OF THE RED DEATH marked the third time you worked with Hazel Court. I'd say here, her character is the most interesting of the three roles, the most morally complex.

CORMAN: Hazel was always very good at playing a femme fatale, if you will. But yes, I think the role of Juliana was interesting because she's a bit more than just the standard villain. She's not wicked, per se. She's

THE MASQUE OF THE RED DEATH

in love. She loves Prospero and wants power so that he will love her more. But Hazel was wonderful and always gave her all. I especially enjoyed shooting the scene where she goes through the ritual of marrying Satan. It gave us the opportunity to repeat the purely cinematic fantasy sequences we had employed in all the Poe pictures, albeit in a much different way. And she was on board for all of it.

ALEXANDER: Are you aware of co-star Jane Asher's most recent career?

CORMAN: I am! Jane is, I'm told, sort of the Martha Stewart of England, known for making cakes. She was a lovely young girl and a very good actress, and she had a quality of innocence that made her a perfect fit for Francesca. I'll tell you another funny little story. She and I used to have lunch together, and one day she introduced me to a friend of hers from Liverpool named Paul. I asked what he did, and he said he was in a singing group, and they were making their debut in London that night. I wished him well. It was of course Paul McCartney, and the next day the headline in the paper read "Beatles Conquer London." They were already the biggest group in England, but I had no idea who they were.

ALEXANDER: THE MASQUE OF THE RED DEATH was originally intended to be your second Poe picture following THE FALL OF THE HOUSE OF USHER, correct?

CORMAN: Yes. That was my original intention after the success of USHER. The problem was that there are many similarities in the story of MASQUE to that of Ingmar Bergman's THE SEVENTH SEAL, a picture I greatly admired at the time from a director I still greatly admire. I was somewhat concerned that if I did THE MASQUE OF THE RED DEATH so close to the recent release of the Bergman picture, I'd be accused of copying it, even though the Poe story was obviously written over a century before!

ALEXANDER: And although you waited, THE MASQUE OF THE RED DEATH nevertheless was still compared to Bergman by many critics.

CORMAN: That's true! But by then, I wasn't terribly concerned about what people thought as we had already created our own identity with the Poe pictures and THE MASQUE OF THE RED DEATH was simply one the best of the remaining tales available to us. And, I had never hidden the fact that for these pictures I was greatly influenced by Bergman and also by Alfred Hitchcock and other European directors.

ALEXANDER: Why did you decide to weave the story of "Hop Frog" into the body of the script?

CORMAN: Chuck Beaumont's script, his original draft, didn't have any element of the "Hop Frog" story at all. That came later into the process of pre-production. What had happened is that I had been

Humiliated by her lover Prospero's waning affections, Juliana schemes.

Francesca and Gino (David Weston) narrowly escape the horror of Prospero's castle.

in Yugoslavia shooting a war picture written by Robert Campbell called THE SECRET INVASION. After that picture wrapped, I immediately went back to London to start THE MASQUE OF THE RED DEATH and when I sat down to re-read Chuck's script, I found that it was missing something, I wasn't sure what. I had gotten quite friendly with Bob and I asked him to have a look at the script and tell me his thoughts. We discussed it and we both agreed that adding "Hop Frog" as a subplot would make the story less thin and give more texture to the picture.

ALEXANDER: It seemed an odd choice to pair Hop Frog — or here, as the character is called, Hop Toad — with a child actor, even though he was played by diminutive adult actor Skip Martin. Why didn't you just cast a dwarf actress in the part?

CORMAN: We tried. That was the original intention. In fact, we interviewed and auditioned many little actresses in London and none of them had that delicate quality that was needed for the part. So instead, we decided to find a young girl and use makeup and costume to make her play older, of course looping her dialogue with an adult voice to make it work. I think visually it works, though it perhaps wasn't as effective as it should have been.

ALEXANDER: Was it a controversial move at all?

CORMAN: I don't think so, particularly. Certainly, some critics noted it and still do. But I don't recall there being any great controversy over the casting.

ALEXANDER: Perhaps due to its British blood, THE MASQUE OF THE RED DEATH is a much less sensational entry in the series, more classical in its approach and certainly in its casting of theatrically trained British actors in supporting roles. What are your memories of working with Patrick Magee?

THE MASQUE OF THE RED DEATH

CORMAN: I adored Patrick. He was a brilliant actor that I had seen in several productions previously and there was just such an aura of grandeur and sense of menace to his presence on screen. I marveled watching him perform. He was able to draw out certain things in the character as written and with just a furrow of his brow or twitch of his lip, he managed to make even the most minor of characters more complete and fully realized. He was truly one of the greats.

ALEXANDER: Vincent's performance is no less flamboyant than it is in previous Poe pictures, but it feels more refined here, if that's the right word.

CORMAN: The thing about Vincent Price is that he was a classically trained actor and an extremely intelligent, well-read individual. And he always took the work seriously. He always gave every part he agreed to do, his all. It didn't matter if it was a horror movie, he didn't give anything less than 100%, whereas some actors might coast through, thinking themselves superior to the material. With the Poe pictures, we were blessed with high quality scripts that gave Vincent ample room to create characters. And with THE MASQUE OF THE DEATH, being surrounded by so many of those seasoned British performers, I believe he was challenged to deliver what became perhaps one of his finest roles in the series, if not his career.

ALEXANDER: The Poe films are genre pictures first and foremost but, if one digs, there's always a dose of potent subtext cannily embedded beneath the surface. In THE MASQUE OF THE RED DEATH, it's even more pronounced and decidedly political. Would you agree?

CORMAN: Yes, that's exactly right. I would refer to it as text and subtext, something I've always employed. For example if you were to make, say, a women in prison picture — and I've made a few of those — you're going to have the elements of a women in prison picture as the text; the subtext is if you have something relevant to say about this subject. And there has to be a statement in there. The statement could be wrong. It's better if it's right, of course, but it's better to have an incorrect statement than to have nothing there at all. It gives complexity to the film that allows you to make some statements you want to make and I think the film becomes a better film for that reason, but you still must recognize on the surface, that the picture is entertainment first.

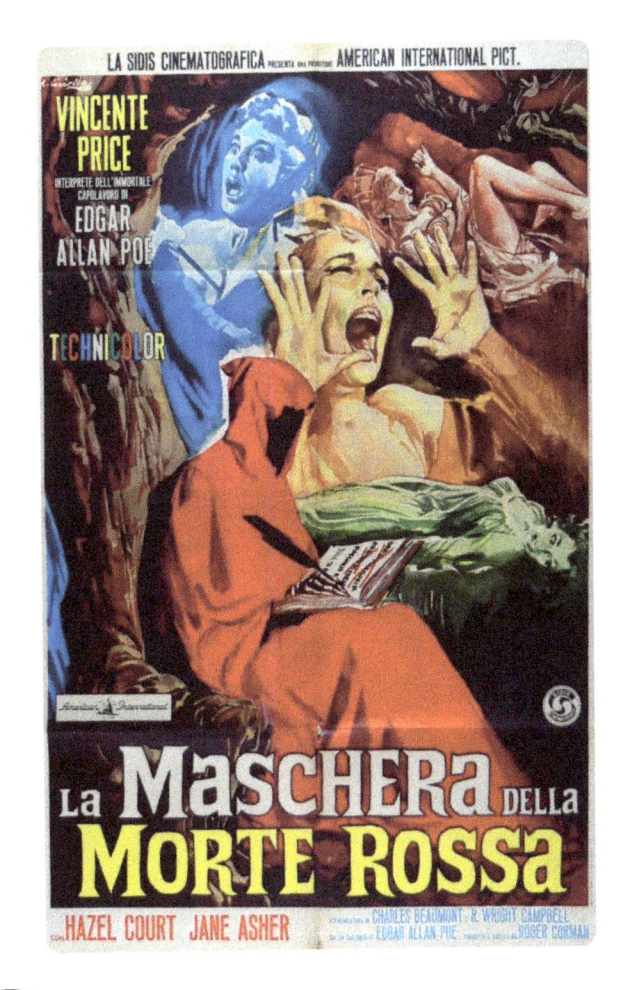

ANALYSIS

Regarded by many as not only the finest entry in the Poe cycle but Corman's crowning directorial achievement, THE MASQUE OF THE RED DEATH is a virtually perfect film. Certainly, it's the most theatrical and literate Poe feature, with endless delicious and often rather daring and cerebral dialogue and pontifications spoken by actors adorned in impossibly lurid costumes, wandering in and around jaw-dropping sets. In fact, MASQUE as written here would make a fantastic stage play. That said, as cinema it's a superlative experience; a fluid, swooning sensorial opera as visualized by Corman, Danny Haller and DP Nicolas Roeg (who goes truly color crazy here; many of the hypnotic visual hallmarks found in his directorial masterworks like DON'T LOOK NOW and BAD TIMING are evident here in their infancy) all powered by David Lee's thundering score. Simply put, THE MASQUE OF THE RED DEATH is a masterpiece.

Price's performance as Prince Prospero is a wonder as well. Though it's generally agreed that his work playing the murderous Matthew Hopkins in Michael Reeves' WITCHFINDER GENERAL is his most restrained and mature latter-day "horror star" turn, MASQUE is just as evolved. In fact, Prospero is a much more dynamic character, a sadistic man of privilege and corrupt class who nevertheless is anchored by his faith and displays genuine affection for Jane Asher's Francesca, a woman whose personal piety matches his own (AIP's post-Corman Gordon Hessler-directed "Poe" film CRY OF THE BANSHEE tries to do to Price's wicked Nobleman what Beaumont, Russell and Corman do with Prospero, but the returns are considerably diminished).

Francesca and Prospero's strange relationship is the odd moral core of THE MASQUE OF THE RED DEATH, suggesting a sort of organic, almost harmonious alliance between good and evil in man and nature, or at least an exemplification of the thin, barely visible line between the two forces, with death (red, in this case) being the equalizer that unites and destroys them both. Even though Prospero burns down her village, murders her father and menaces her lover and despite Prospero's fervent Satanism running diametrically counter to her devout Christianity, Francesca has obvious feelings for Prospero, recognizing the humanity he keeps carefully hidden from his subjects and underlings. Asher rarely gets

THE MASQUE OF THE RED DEATH

Prospero's fate is reflected in the face of The Red Death.

the accolades she deserves for this complex portrayal, and she matches Price's presence, standing toe-to-toe and never letting his intensity (some might say hamminess) overpower their scenes together.

Everything just works here. The supporting cast of theatrically trained British actors add heft to every single scene, especially Magee and Corman regular Court who both ooze malevolence and sexual decadence. Skip Martin also gives a fully realized performance as Hop Toad, the smallest — and perhaps smartest — man in the court, meticulously plotting the grisliest of vengeance against the man who humiliated his lover. The color-coded plague wraiths that wander the misty, disease-choked countryside are mysterious and eerie and that frenzied, eloquent, stylized and bloody climax is unforgettable.

Once more, Corman enlists the aid of dynamic credits sequences, the opening with its fonts pushing thorn-like tendrils into the screen and its closing credit Tarot deck coolness signing off with the greatest final moment in the series' entire run.

While THE PIT AND THE PENDULUM may be my favorite of Roger's Poe films, MASQUE is probably the best of them, worthy of every accolade lauded upon it. It functions as a horror movie, sure. But it defies the parameters of genre. Like THE FALL OF THE HOUSE OF USHER, Corman and his crew manage to make something approaching the highbrow and yet consistently crack the whip revealing broad strokes of pulpy sadism and perversity. It's a costume drama, a morality fable, a kinky love story, a philosophical parable, an action film (it's the only entry in the Poe cycle that features a protracted sword fight!) and the blackest of comedies. It's everything cinema should be and so much more.

THE TOMB OF LIGEIA

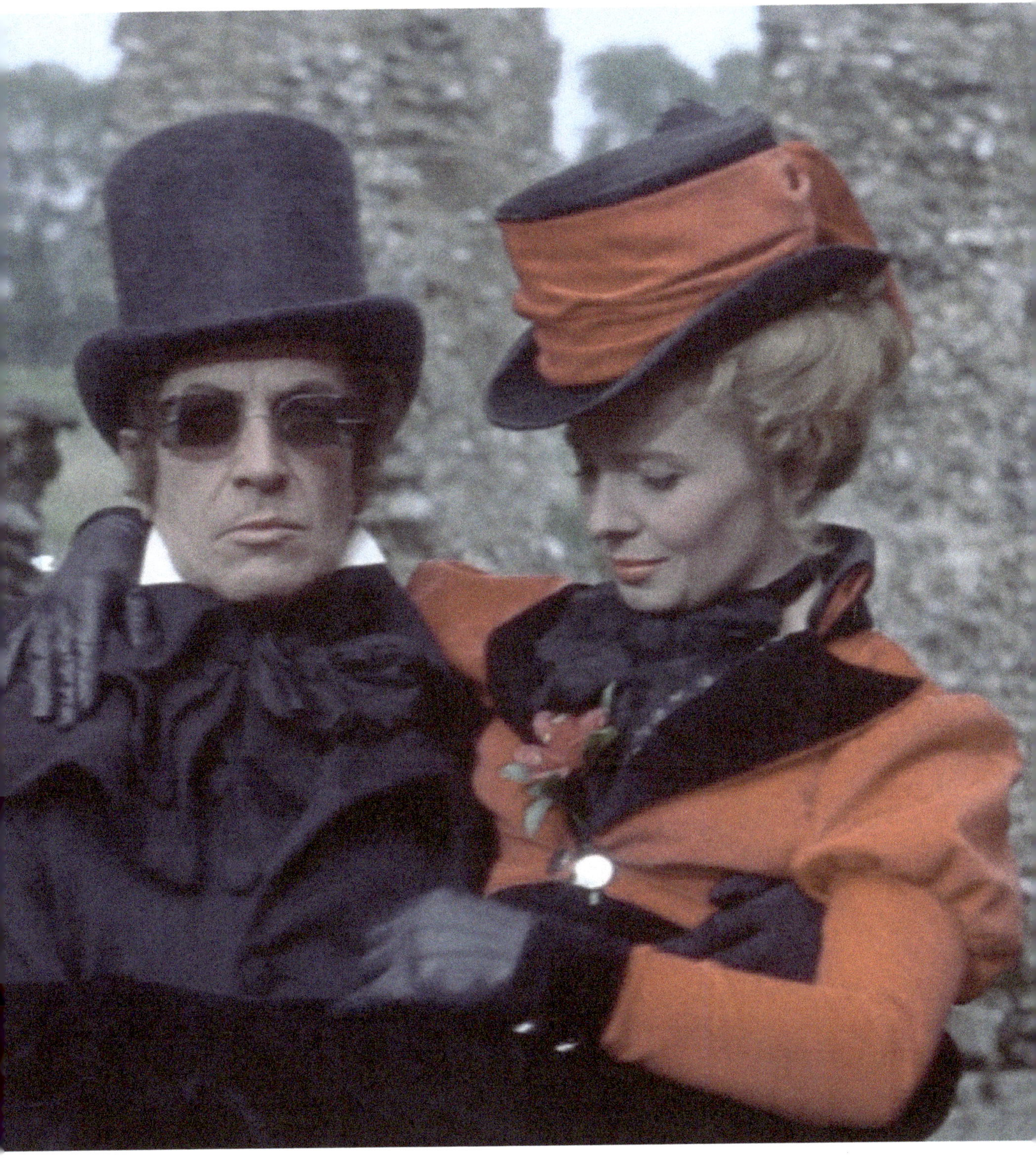

CORMAN/POE

CAST
Vincent Price as Verden Fell
Elizabeth Shepherd as Lady Rowena Trevanion / Lady Ligeia
John Westbrook as Christopher Gough
Derek Francis as Lord Trevanion
Oliver Johnston as Kenrick
Richard Vernon as Dr. Vivian
Frank Thornton as Peperel
Ronald Adam as The Minister
Denis Gilmore as The Livery Boy
Penelope Lee as The Maidservant

WRITTEN
Charles Beaumont & R. Wright Campbell
Based on the story "THE TOMB OF LIGEIA"
by Edgar Allan Poe

MUSIC
Kenneth V. Jones

CINEMATOGRAPHY
Arthur Grant

EDITED
Alfred Cox

PRODUCTION DESIGN
Daniel Haller & Colin Southcott

SPECIAL EFFECTS
Ted Samuels

PRODUCED
Samuel Z. Arkoff, James H. Nicholson,
David Deutsch (uncredited), Pat Green
& Roger Corman

DIRECTED
Roger Corman

SYNOPSIS

Through the ruins of a crumbling abbey, a funeral procession moves, black-suited pallbearers carrying a wooden coffin with a window on its lid. Inside lies Ligeia Fell, beautiful in death as she was in life, raven haired, porcelain skin and a look of calm on her alabaster face. A minister emerges from a carriage, balking at the deceased being buried in the consecrated ground of the cemetery, citing the dead woman sealed in the box as a non-Christian.

Her crestfallen husband, Verden Fell claims the ground as his and ignores the holy man's protests. Fell defiantly states that before her passing, Ligeia willed herself not to die. Suddenly, a black cat pounces on the coffin lid, the disturbance causing Ligeia's muscles to spasm and her eyes jolt open. As they lower the dead woman into the ground, the camera pans up to the headstone, where the cat rests.

Sometime later, we see a fox running for its life as a traditional English hunt is afoot. Breaking free from the pack, Lady Rowena Trevanion steers her horse into Fell's ruins, inexplicably drawn to Ligeia's stone. After uttering the dead woman's name, the screeching black cat appears again, frightening Rowena's horse and knocking her to the ground. Seeing the inky feline perched on the grave, she gets up and smilingly reaches for it when suddenly Verden appears in top hat and black sunglasses, shocking her into a scream. Her fellow hunter and friend Christopher Gough hears the shriek and investigates, where he encounters Fell who stands vigil by the now unconscious Rowena. Christopher is surprised to see Verden, who due to his reclusive nature he had presumed dead. Rowena wakes and after being introduced to Fell, and falling immediately under his spell, plucks a flower from Ligeia's grave and pins it to her coat. Verden picks the still fragile Rowena up and carries her to his home while Christopher rides to fetch the lady's father. Rowena is fascinated by Fell and, after inquiring about his bizarre four-sided black glasses, she learns that the Nobleman has a sensitivity to the sun, his eyesight so acute that without the aid of the glasses he's forced to live by night. Inside the abbey, Fell instructs his servant Heinrich to fetch sherry and bandages, removing the woman's shoe and binding her sprained ankle.

Christopher's father, the boorish Lord Trevanian and Christopher arrive, the now dead fox in a basket. After informing the pair that his late wife once kept a fox as a pet, Trevanian is shocked to learn that his

The curse of Ligeia commences (L-R: Vincent Price, Elizabeth Shepherd, John Westbrook).

trophy has vanished, a theft Fell blames on the black cat that perpetually prowls the grounds. As they ride off together, Rowena questions Christopher about Fell and he explains how dramatically different a man his former friend has become since the death of Ligeia. The next day, over breakfast at the Trevanian estate, a servant delivers a document to Christopher on behalf of Fell, to which the lawyer signs and orders the servant to return. Rowena steals the document with the intention of delivering it to Verden herself. When she arrives at the desolate abbey, Fell sees Rowena in silhouette and, thinking her to be the spirit of Ligeia, attacks her. When he realizes his error, he apologies while simultaneously scolding her for coming to his home unannounced. After calming down, Fell offers to make tea for the frightened woman but Rowena, still fascinated by what she sees as an enticingly enigmatic man, takes the task on herself and the pair sit together in Fell's filthy kitchen. As they begin to get comfortable together, Fell suddenly stiffens and insists Rowena leave, proclaiming himself to be a broken man, obsessed and damaged by the figurative (or perhaps literal) ghost of his dead wife. When Rowena tenderly reaches to touch Fell's cheek, the black cat appears again and scratches Rowena's face. Fell orders Kenrick to find and destroy the cat.

THE TOMB OF LIGEIA

Christopher appears at the home to visit his friend and he and Fell walk into the courtyard, stopping at Ligeia's grave. The morose man explains that after Rowena's arrival, the date of death from Ligeia's stone mysteriously vanished. When Christopher inquires as to why only Ligeia's death date was etched on the marker, Fell claims that he never really knew Ligeia's true age. As Fell continues to speak on his wife's final days and his suspicions that he is losing his mind, Rowena walks through the house, picking up her fallen hat while the black cat watches and absconds with Fell's sunglasses. Rowena fearlessly follows the cat, deep into the dark of the house, up stone stairs to the peak of the bell tower. Suddenly, the bell begins to toll, pummeling Rowena with sound, sending her into hysterics.

Hearing the noise and Rowena's terrified screams, Fell runs back into the abbey, rescuing the lady and, after embracing her, tells her she is safe with him.

Time passes and the bell tolls anew, this time as Verden and Rowena emerge from the church as husband and wife. As their carriage whisks them away to their honeymoon, Christopher looks on ruefully, clearly crestfallen that the woman he loved is lost to another.

Weeks later, as the couple return home, Fell tells Rowena that he has arranged for Christopher to sell the abbey and that they will be moving away to a new home. That night, Rowena prepares for bed in her chamber and she is startled by what sounds like hair being brushed. She gets up and walks over to her vanity to see jet black hair embedded in her brush. The next morning, over breakfast with Christopher and Rowena's father, Christopher informs Verden that the deed to the abbey is still in Ligeia's name, and they can find no death certificate, a fact that is legally hampering the sale. The conversation then drifts to the ethereal, with Verden discussing the controversial new pseudo-science of mesmerism. Rowena agrees to let her husband attempt to hypnotize her. Under Verden's suggestive spell, Rowena talks of her mother and a song she would sing to her as a child. Rowena sings the song when suddenly her voice changes and eyes open, her face now steely and grim as she embodies the persona of the dead Ligeia. The possessed Rowena looks directly at Fell and swears that she will always be his wife, before passing out.

Rowena is put to bed, exhausted, and she begs Verden to stay with her before falling into a deep sleep. Her dreams are fevered, a miasma of distorted images: a dead fox bleeding at the mouth; a black cat attacking. She sees herself in slow motion wandering long corridors towards an open armed Verden, who passionately kisses her, pulling his head back to reveal the smiling face of the raven haired Ligeia. Rowena wakes in terror only to find the dead fox from her dream lying on top of her chest, a gift from the perpetually stalking cat.

The next morning over breakfast, Rowena confesses to Christopher that she sleeps alone and eats alone and that she truly believes that Ligeia IS alive, haunting the house and unable to let Verden go. That night, Christopher confronts Kenrick, demanding to know the truth about Ligeia. The servant is visibly nervous and says very little, apparently frightened of what his master might do to him if he talks. As the night wears on, Christopher and a pair of men exhume Ligeia's grave while a storm brews.

Inside, the black cat relentlessly pursues Rowena around the house and when a mirror smashes, a hidden room is revealed. At the same time, Christopher exhumes Ligeia's coffin and there, behind the glass

CORMAN/POE

Elizabeth Shepherd as Ligeia, the darker half of a delicious double role.

window, her body lies, perfectly preserved. But when his torch falls onto the glass, breaking it, the body catches fire; the body is in fact a wax replica of Ligeia.

Inside, Rowena encounters Verden in the hidden room and discovers Ligeia's actual corpse, perfectly preserved, lying on her black bed. Exhausted and in shock, he falls onto the body. Suddenly, Christopher and Kenrick appear, urging Rowena to come with them. Kenrick states that Ligeia's supernatural spectral will has placed Verden in a sort of perpetual state of hypnosis and that only Ligeia can release him. But as Ligeia is no longer among the actual living, the spell can never break.

Rowena attempts to impersonate Ligeia and hypnotically talks Verden out of his trance, causing her to faint, though the ruse works, and Verden is released. Verden walks towards the body of his dead first wife, picking up her near-mummified body and throwing it into the fireplace. He then carries Rowena's body to Ligeia's bed and kisses her on the lips, and, thinking her dead, gently covers her body in a sheet. The cat appears on her corpse and Rowena begins to breathe. Slowly, the shroud slips away and there on the bed, in place of Rowena, lies the raven haired Ligeia. Verden lunges for her throat, choking her, and when Christopher yells at him to stop, he sees that he is in fact choking Rowena. Disoriented, he begs Christopher to take her away and then sets off to kill the omnipresent cat, the vessel that now houses Ligeia's monstrous spirit. The beast jumps on his face and claws out his eyes. Now blinded, Verden stumbles through the room, accidentally knocking over a pillar that lands in the fireplace, instantly setting the room ablaze. As the flames engulf the walls, Verden tries to find his way out but is consumed by the blaze. Before he is incinerated, he catches the cat and manages to strangle it to death.

In the carriage outside, Rowena wakes up in Christopher's arms while Verden burns, lying beside the body of Ligeia, now fully transformed to her true self in this, the moment of her final, true death.

"The boundaries which divide life from death are at best shadowy and vague. Who shall say where the one ends and the other begins?" — Poe

INTERVIEW: ROGER CORMAN ON THE TOMB OF LIGEIA

ALEXANDER: Like THE MASQUE OF THE RED DEATH, THE TOMB OF LIGEIA was also shot in England but TOMB has a radically different look and feel, separate from any of the pictures.

CORMAN: It does. As I have mentioned, I had specific theories on how to do the films, and they changed as I moved from picture to picture. By the time we got to THE TOMB OF LIGEIA, I just wanted to vary the visuals. My feeling was always that with the Poe films, I was working primarily with the unconscious mind, and I wanted to stay away as much as possible from the real exterior world; when I did show the real world, I went to the ocean or a burned-out forest, to make it somewhat unreal. Uncanny. But for THE TOMB OF LIGEIA I went right into the countryside in broad daylight. And that wasn't really for any other reason than I personally wanted to make a break from the others. They were all starting to look alike. Even though the mood and themes of THE TOMB OF LIGEIA are in line with some of the other Poe pictures, I thought that taking the story and the action out into the beautiful English sunshine, with those green hills, the ruins and natural environment was the change the series needed, and I just make it all a primarily exterior sort of aesthetic.

ALEXANDER: And Grant was blessed by those locations, I think. That ruined abbey is indeed marvelously cinematic.

CORMAN: Vincent and I had talked about this often during our frequent collaborations on the Poe pictures, about how great it would be to shoot in actual ruins and I think having the chance to do so really invigorated both of us.

ALEXANDER: How did you find it?

CORMAN: During pre-production, I had rented a car to drive around the countryside, from London all through Wales and almost up to Scotland, with the intent on finding the perfect location. And I finally found it in Norfolk, with the interiors being shot in Shepperton studios, an excellent studio outside of London. And I really think when you watch the picture, even now, the cutting between the set and the ruined castle exteriors is virtually flawless.

ALEXANDER: For those interiors, you once more employed Daniel Haller.

CORMAN: Yes, Danny was a constant in the Poe pictures.

CORMAN/POE

The vengeful spirit of Ligeia takes hold of Lady Rowena (Shepherd) while Christopher recoils.

ALEXANDER: Because this was a more exterior-based film, set in and around those ruins, did you and Danny discuss a different look to the interior of the set?

CORMAN: We did as there had to be a visual and textural match to those exteriors on the Shepperton set, more gray and desaturated, less reds, more blues. We spaced things out more, using wide angle lenses again to make the set look larger and Danny and I used a lot of foreground and background composition, sort of moving in and around and behind the Egyptian statues and various props that Vincent's character had in the home. It was, as usual, a marvelous set that Danny built. I remember that there was a large doorway in the middle of the main room of the set, a door that sat above a staircase. Now, the door wasn't actually a door at all. It didn't open and didn't lead anywhere; it was only a visual part of the set. I remember constantly having to cheat that, to make it look like Vincent was entering and exiting that door. In one scene John Westbrook is holding a prop in the foreground of a shot, examining it and blocking the doorway. I then moved the head of the prop down to reveal what looked like Vincent closing the door behind him and ascending the stairs. It worked very well and we got away with it.

ALEXANDER: In your previous British Poe picture, THE MASQUE OF THE RED DEATH, your cameraman was Nicolas Roeg. Here you employed Arthur Grant, a veteran of Hammer Films.

CORMAN: Yes, Nicholas, who was an excellent young cameraman, had moved on at this point and was well on his way to becoming a fine director and I couldn't use Floyd Crosby again, as due to the rules of the British tax law, we had to use a primarily British crew and I had already brought Danny with me. So, we used Arthur who was a very talented and very

THE TOMB OF LIGEIA

seasoned cameraman. He was particularly good at shooting the daylight exteriors, though I felt the day for night shots weren't as successful as in some of my other pictures. At that point, the English weren't quite as good as the Americans at shooting day for night, for whatever reason. It might have something to do with the perpetual English fog that diminishes the sunlight as you need very bright daylight to get proper day for night. But Arthur was excellent at working with Danny to make the sets look much larger than they were, using various lenses and compositions and I feel like the film breathes a bit more than the others, due in no small part to Arthur's work.

ALEXANDER: The Poe films often employed the use of matte shots but here you abandoned those entirely.

CORMAN: Not entirely, actually, no. The difference in THE TOMB OF LIGEIA is that we used those mattes sparingly. In some of the earlier pictures, we held shots featuring matte paintings for prolonged periods and sometimes I feel they called attention to themselves. But here, we used them and cut quickly away from them, so the audience didn't have the time to acknowledge them. They are there occasionally. Just not as pronounced.

ALEXANDER: Vincent's look as Verden Fell is iconic. With those glasses and that cloak and top hat…

CORMAN: Yes, he does have a very striking look in the picture. Although the character of Fell as written was actually supposed to be a bit younger, or at least more of a romantic leading man part and Vincent was at this point much older. We had to put considerably more make-up on him than usual and place a kind of filter on the lens that softened his look, an effect usually reserved for actresses. But he pulled it off. I've said it before to you and to others, but Vincent really was wonderful on every level, a wonderful actor and a commanding presence with a unique, almost regal intensity. It didn't matter how old he was, he made the part his own.

ALEXANDER: You've also said before that Ray Milland was initially considered for the role, who is certainly a bit more of a subdued and romantic lead, as evidenced in THE PREMATURE BURIAL.

CORMAN: Well, no, Ray wasn't really seriously considered for the part, I should clarify this. As I say, I was somewhat initially concerned about Vincent's age and how well it works in the picture and for a moment, I did contemplate Ray and wonder if he might be a better fit. Ray wasn't much younger than Vincent, but

I did feel he may have had a more youthful look. But that was only a fleeting thought as I knew Vincent would bring a complexity to his performance that the character needed. And I was right.

ALEXANDER: Elizabeth Shepherd is marvelous in the film.

CORMAN: Elizabeth was an exceptional woman. A beautiful, strong actress who went on to have a fine career. This was her first lead role, if I recall correctly. She was very young but there was a maturity to her face and her manner, making her play slightly older than she was. Vincent was considerably older than Elizabeth, but I feel that her sophistication and intelligent portrayal was able to match him and make that age difference less noticeable. She was also very expressive, especially during sequences with minimal dialogue; she was very good at conveying emotion physically. So again, we had Vincent, who was a bit too old for the role, and Elizabeth who was a bit too young. And they met in the middle and made it work!

ALEXANDER: And like Vincent had done previously in THE PIT AND THE PENDULUM and THE HAUNTED PALACE, Elizabeth plays two characters here, the light and the dark, good and evil.

CORMAN: Yes, and flawlessly, I might add, though it's debatable if the actual character of Ligeia is even a fully realized character. There's a great scene in the picture where Vincent has sort of hypnotized Elizabeth by the fire, where she lapses into her other persona and she did that effortlessly, completely changing her face and expression and tone of voice before reverting to herself. It was a marvelous performance to watch and I remember the crew and I applauded after we cut.

ALEXANDER: Many critics claim THE TOMB OF LIGEIA is the most accomplished of the Poe films. Do you agree?

CORMAN: I will say that I like the film a lot, primarily because of the script, an excellent one by Robert Towne, who later became quite big and winner of several Academy Awards.

ALEXANDER: What was it specifically about Towne's script that you liked?

CORMAN: Bob understands character, the psychology of character and how, shall we say, damaged or psychologically tormented people relate to each other. There's something very believable in his characters, despite the fantastical things going on around them. And there's an intelligence and subtlety to his dialogue. It was just a very, very good script, a love story in many respects, and it was very clear even then that Bob would go on to have great success in Hollywood.

ALEXANDER: Why was THE TOMB OF LIGEIA the final entry in the cycle? It seemed as though, with the new locations and evolving visual aesthetic, you could have kept going with them.

CORMAN: If it were up to AIP, 3131 would have kept going. They wanted me to make more of them. At one point, it was discussed that the next picture would be an adaptation of THE GOLD BUG.

ALEXANDER: Was Vincent intended for the lead?

CORMAN: Yes, and I believe he wanted to do it. But I said, no, that's it. Comedy, bigger sets, outdoor, countryside exteriors or not, I really thought I'd run out of ideas and that they were all just repeating themselves. And you know, this was the sixties,

THE TOMB OF LIGEIA

Lady Rowena draws back the drapes to reveal the ultimate horror.

then moving into the late sixties and it was the time of the counterculture and I wanted to get out and photograph what was going on in the streets, to feel the energy of youth. And the first picture I made right after THE TOMB OF LIGEIA was THE WILD ANGELS, which was of course about the Hell's Angels motorcycle gang that was the opposite of the sort of studio-bound work I was doing. AIP went on to make more Poe pictures later on, with different directors and many starring Vincent.

ALEXANDER: When you saw this wave of latter-period AIP Poe films, did you ever have even a pang of regret about abandoning the cycle?

CORMAN: None at all. I had honestly said all I had to say and had happily moved on by that point.

ALEXANDER: How about leaving AIP? Were you always confident you made the right decision?

CORMAN: Yes. As I've said, my years at AIP were happy ones and Sam and Jim gave me considerable freedom. But I remember after I made THE WILD ANGELS and THE TRIP, both counter-culture films that were very well reviewed and very successful. THE WILD ANGELS was the opening night picture at the Venice Film Festival and THE TRIP premiered at Cannes. However, AIP had tampered with them somewhat, slightly editing a few key scenes without my knowledge. At this point I understood the business, and I wanted to start my own company, partly to ensure no one did that to me again.

ALEXANDER: Today it is unlikely that younger audiences would connect with dialogue-heavy period-piece horror shows; why do you think they gravitated toward them back then?

CORMAN: For a number of reasons. We were still at the beginning of television; motion pictures were still dominant, and people were still being taught classical English in school, and I believe people were just more literate. Also, I might add one other thing — and this just occurred to me — people were more interested in the past. I would bet that if someone did a survey of the percentage of historical films made before the 1960s and the percentage afterward, you would find that the percentage of historical, classical films was higher before the 1960s. The youth revolution of the '60s moved people away from history to more immediate, contemporary events. I just thought of this theory this very second, and I can't back it up in any way, but it sounds logical to me so I'll roll with it!

ANALYSIS

Roger's series swan song is indeed an elegant, decidedly mature and even — despite its lurid, sensational subject matter — a delicate work of Gothic drama. It's no wonder he dropped the microphone on Poe after this; it's difficult to believe he could have topped it, at least without cycling back to earlier entries and repeating himself, something he was constantly trying not to do. That said, THE TOMB OF LIGEIA's relative restraint might disappoint some disciples who prefer the hyperbolic psychosis of THE PIT AND THE PENDULUM or the Shakespeare from Hell, oration-heavy theatrics of THE MASQUE OF THE RED DEATH. Instead, we get a mannered portrait of a death-fixated neurotic who has fully isolated himself from society, haunted — either literally or figuratively — by the specter of his dead wife. Fell is a man who punishes himself for having even an ounce of hope, living in constant terror that anything good that comes his way will perish and open his barely healed wounds. He's got PTSD, has built high emotional walls around himself and any sort of supernatural shenanigans that claw at the peripherals of the plot can subjectively be read as ambiguities, as allegorical, not literal manifestations. On that level, Robert Towne's screenplay is absolutely the most sophisticated and mature of any of the Poe films, its dialogue infused with a sort of poetry and its pace measured and macabre. It's the apex of the series in that sense.

And yet, THE TOMB OF LIGEIA suffers somewhat by sacrificing that saturated sense of pulp fun that propelled other entries. While I cited THE HAUNTED PALACE as being relatively humorless, it was still amusing; it still had plenty of black humor as it went all the way with its single-minded Grand Guignol, oppressive atmosphere and ludicrous, melodramatic mayhem. THE TOMB OF LIGEIA is not funny at all. There's nothing here to laugh at. It's even more chained to highbrow literary affectation than THE FALL OF THE HOUSE OF USHER. It's a respectable, mature penny dreadful, evocative and lyrical, especially with its earthy, wide backdrop that makes it feel in some stretches almost like a western.

Towne's unsentimental, understated screenplay feels like it's moving closer to the sort of American New Wave style of cinema that he would become such an instrumental part of. There's a lack of moral judgment here, a refusal to cast any sort of stone. Rather, Towne

THE TOMB OF LIGEIA

Verdun and Christopher panic as the woman they both love collapses.

simply essays a crisp, clinical, eye-level view of the world as it exists.

It's no wonder Corman left the Poe pictures behind after this, moving into the more urgent verité of the film reflecting the burgeoning counterculture. THE TOMB OF LIGEIA feels like the work of a filmmaker literally spreading his wings, leaving one world and feathering a nest in something new, a picture standing on either side of the meridian of the zeitgeist shift. A work that perhaps subconsciously is breaking free from a set-bound, designer — or as Roger calls it, interior — world into the beauty of the natural world and examining its effect on the individual.

Which is not to say THE TOMB OF LIGEIA is totally at odds with the cycle. Rather it's a sort of fitting finale, an epitaph, a coda. But it's still very much built on the bones of the early Matheson and Beaumont scripted pictures, of the American-lensed productions and even of the glamourous pomp of the previous British-made film. Fell is very much a healthier incarnation of Roderick Usher, of the classic doomed Poe hero. A man who wants to climb out of the domestic tomb he has built for himself brick by miserable, melancholic brick, but who simply cannot snap free of the past. Fell is just as tormented a figure as Nicholas Medina, a victim teetering on the edge of sanity. He is as cynical as Guy Carrell or as bitter and isolated as Locke. He's just — as written and then performed by Price — more accepting of his situation. When Elizabeth enters his world, she distracts him and offers him a glimmer of hope that a future free of crushing sadness and guilt might exist, that a fresh, clean kind of love might wash off the stain — either psychological or supernatural — that his former romance has left on his mind and body. And like all doomed Poe protagonists, he soon finds out that prophecies are self-fulfilled, and the past will never, ever let go. And that sometimes it's more noble to be erased than spread your psychic sickness to anyone else.

APPENDIX

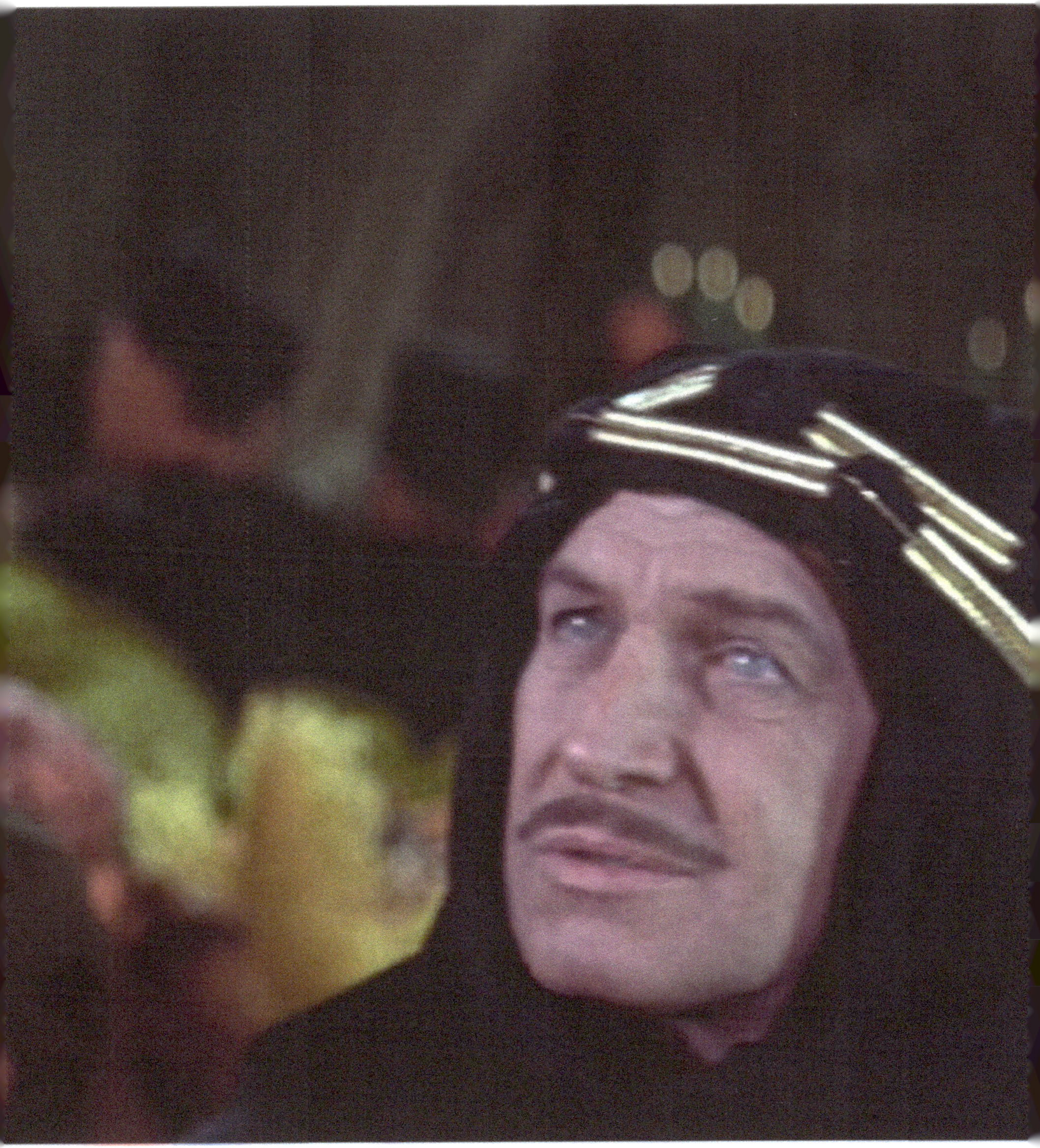

THE CENSORING OF THE MASQUE OF THE RED DEATH

The following scans of original documents were kindly provided to me for use here by veteran film producer, archivist, restorationist and Corman alumnus Jon Davison. These letters and memos chart the pressure American International Pictures was under leading up to the release of the film, both by The Catholic Legion of Decency (aka The National Legion of Decency) as well as the British Board of Film Classification (BBFC). Thanks to the efforts of Davison, fellow archivist and Corman disciple Joe Dante and various other film collectors from around the globe, the fully restored, uncensored version of THE MASQUE OF THE RED DEATH is now widely available.

PICTURED RIGHT: A letter from American International Pictures executive Al Simms (on official AIP letterhead) to Rev. Patrick J. Sullivan, Assistant Executive Secretary of The Catholic Legion of Decency dated June 10th, 1964, regarding anticipatory cuts the studio had made to THE MASQUE OF THE RED DEATH in order to hopefully gain The Legion's approval.

PAGES 128 & 129: A memo from The Catholic Legion of Decency film reviewer Father Sal Miraliotta to AIP dated June 15th, 1964 in which Miraliotta critically itemizes what he — on behalf of The Legion — deems to be offensive and objectionable about the THE MASQUE OF THE RED DEATH as a whole and, in the process, changes his initial suggested rating of "B" (meaning "objectionable in part for all") to the dreaded "C" ("condemned").

THE CENSORING OF
THE MASQUE OF THE RED DEATH

American International Pictures
A CALIFORNIA CORPORATION
7165 SUNSET BLVD. • HOLLYWOOD 46, CALIFORNIA
HOLLYWOOD 6-3311 • CABLE: AMERPIX

AL SIMMS
DIRECTOR OF
MUSIC & PERSONNEL

June 10, 1964

Reverend Patrick J. Sullivan, S.J., S.T.D.
Assistant Executive Secretary
NATIONAL LEGION OF DECENCY
453 Madison Avenue
New York 22, New York

Dear Father Sullivan:

As per our telephone conversation, I am shipping the cuts on MASQUE OF THE RED DEATH to Mr. Billitteri and he will show them to you the day you screen the picture.

As I told you, Monsignor Little has informed us that it would be impossible for him to screen MASQUE OF THE RED DEATH prior to his leaving for Europe, so I proceeded to make cuts which in my estimation should be made in order to give us an equitable rating on the picture. I am very happy that we will be able to screen this for you now inasmuch as the picture is booked for a June 24th opening.

With respect to the rating on UNDER AGE, I want you to know that I am in complete disagreement with The Legion on this picture and I will discuss it further with you and the Monsignor when we meet in Italy.

Thank you for your cooperation. God bless you. Until I see you in Europe, my kindest personal regards. Have a good flight.

Sincerely,

Al Simms

AS/j

cc: Mr. James H. Nicholson
    Mr. Samuel Z. Arkoff
    Mr. David J. Melamed
    Mr. Salvator Billitteri

NO AGREEMENT WILL BE BINDING ON THIS CORPORATION UNLESS IN WRITING AND SIGNED BY A CORPORATE OFFICER

SJM:LD   June 18, 1964

National Legion of Decency
New York City: Week of June 15, 1964

<u>Masque Of The Red Death</u>:- Last Monday, after the screening, I phoned in a Class "B" rating on this film. The comments are following now.

It is valid for any creative author to take a first rate short story and embellish it into a full length screen play. A responsible author will attempt to do justice to the ~~original~~ original teller of the tale. Some authors---such as is the case here...out-imagine the original teller and create a new story of their own. In so doing, authors Beaumont and Campbell have done Poe a disservice, especially in the conclusions of those who know nothing or may have forgotten what little they did know about that great master of tales of terror and imagination. Incidentally, this ignorance could well be dispelled or placed in proper perspective should they re-read Poe or begin to read him and then read that ~~he~~ biography of Poe, "Israfel" by Hervey Allen. This surfices as a starter.

What our screenwriters, who show considerable talent and skill with words, have done here is to have a played a trick on the viewers. While they have kept Poe's characters and, to a good extent, descriptions, they also have added(or borrowed from other sources) a theme of Satanic worship and saturated it with a ~~quintessence~~ quintessence of evil doings and dialogue....a fact that is not in the original story at all. It is in fact a thorough development of the word Poe used: the "wanton" aspect Poe ascribed to Prospero and his court. But Poe was spinning a tale of death and corruption of the body(a theme close to him). Here our authors are treating of spiritual corruption, the malignancy of the soul, the evil of humanity; of a corrupt court in bizarre surroundings and macabre circumstnaces.

Now, within the scope of literature, I think we can admit this, even though it repulses us as we see the Christian Mass defiled. At least we can say there is a basis in fact for these evil doings...by this I mean there ~~practitioners are practitioners~~ are practitioners of the Black Mass and worshipers of the Prince of Darkness.

The trick played by our screenwirters is that they have not written an original work, hence casting reflection upon their seriousness of purpose which would sanction validity of theme. And also, they have ~~composed a story really, but merely stringing together~~ not composed a story really, but merely strung together a series of phrases and ~~gibberish~~ gibberish for effect. There is some mumbo-jumbo Latin which is a travesty on words and rites used by the priest. We hear "Prince of Darkness" and we think of J.F.Powers, but with little justice, I should say, to that marvelous writer. Some words of Poe are used, but Poe did not write a story a Satanism, such as this is. The film pretends to be serious and often enough times it does reach a level of strong drama, even as it does have a powerful and theatrically effective climax. But careful attention reveals an added attraction, so to speak.

more

THE CENSORING OF THE MASQUE OF THE RED DEATH

SJM:LD:Week of June 15, 1964   p.2

Not only is the film out and out Satanism in theme, it also is, through its costuming, potent ~~criticism~~ eroticism. Under ordinary circumstances, such costuming would be a revealing thing with its expected sensual appeal. But as done here, it achieves an ~~added dimension~~ added dimension, especially when Miss Court enacts scenes and speaks of ~~m~~arriage with the devil. Here there is charged-up Faustian glee that results in a hyper-sexual connotation. Now, not all viewers may see this; they may just regard this as a crazy way-out story. I should say that such interpretations will be closer to those (and there are many of us) who appreciate worthy tales of terror and the supernatural. But no matter how dull, I doubt that anyone will fail to see the eroticism of the costuming in this story. We could give the screenwriters a benefit and allow them their visual manifestations of wantoness and debauchery. But I also say they should not discredit Poe even with the broadest interpretation of the phrase "based on...". Because if the discredit ended here, it would be enough for our objection. But it goes even further: the film is not only a travesty of Christian worship, it also renders the concept of Christianity ineffectual and useless. Precisely how the story resolves itself escapes me at the moment. I recall something that the only good or bad in people is of an earthly nature and that death is all for all. But I do know that the film makes no offer in the earthly positive or theologically supernatural direction. Perhaps the authors were so intense in emphasizing evil for its own sake, that they considered it would be soundly dramatic to keep hammering away at this idea without a "happy ending" switch. If this is what they had in mind they succeeded admirably. Too admirably, in fact, because they could have made their point without defiling the thoughts and beliefs of Christians. So that, in telling a tale of death, they did not stick to the subject. They made points for the devil. And so, having written these thoughts out, I change my rating to:

                    Class "C"

      more

CORMAN/POE

American International
PICTURES
AMERICAN INTERNATIONAL EXPORT CORPORATION
NEW YORK OFFICE: 165 WEST 46TH STREET · NEW YORK 36 N.Y.
CIRCLE 5-3035   CABLE ADDRESS: EXAMERIC

June 22, 1964

Rev. Patrick J. Sullivan, S.J., S.T.D.
National Legion of Decency
453 Madison Avenue
New York 22, New York

Re: "MASQUE OF THE RED DEATH"

Dear Father Sullivan:

This is to confirm that as per our understanding I have made the three (3) cuts in the picture and track negatives of the above film.

REEL 1A: Illusion of nudity as girl is falling into bath-tub has been eliminated;

REEL 4A: The dialogue spoken by Juliana "Alleluia" has been cut out of the track negative;

REEL 5A: The dialogue spoken by the Man In Red "his own God for himself" has been eliminated in the track negative together with the corresponding picture.

Kindest personal regards.

Sincerely yours,
AMERICAN INTERNATIONAL PICTURES

Salvatore Billitteri

SB:cr
cc: Messrs. Nicholson
    Arkoff
    Simms
    Zide
    Golden

ALL OFFERS SUBJECT TO PRIOR SALE OR WITHDRAWAL — AN OFFER DOES NOT CONSTITUTE A CONTRACT

After much presumed back and forth between American International Pictures and The Catholic Legion of Decency regarding their condemnation of THE MASQUE OF THE RED DEATH, AIP executive Salvatore Billitteri itemizes cuts the studio has made to the film in order to gain The Legion's reluctant approval in this letter dated June 22nd, 1964.

THE CENSORING OF
THE MASQUE OF THE RED DEATH

MOTION PICTURE ASSOCIATION
OF AMERICA, INC.
8480 BEVERLY BOULEVARD
HOLLYWOOD 48, CALIFORNIA
OLIVE 3-2200

CONFIDENTIAL

THE FOLLOWING IS A COPY OF REPORT, RECEIVED FROM THE LOCAL CENSOR BOARD, IN THE TERRITORY NAMED, ON THE PICTURE TITLED:

FEATURE	COMPANY	TERRITORY
MASQUE OF THE RED DEATH	AMERICAN INT'L	BRITISH MAY 1964

DELETIONS:

REEL 1   REDUCE SHOTS OF PERSON ON FIRE.
REDUCE SHOTS AND DIALOGUE SHOWING ALFREDO'S INTEREST IN THE FEMALE DWARF.

D. REEL 2   REMOVE ALL SHOTS AND DIALOGUE IN WHICH SCARLATTI OFFERS HIS WIFE TO PROSPERO IN RETURN FOR ADMITTANCE TO THE CASTLE, AND PROSPERO'S REPLY "I HAVE ALREADY HAD THAT DOUBTFUL PLEASURE."
THE WHOLE SCENE IN WHICH GIULIANA OFFERS HERSELF TO THE DEVIL SHOULD BE REMOVED.

D. REEL 3   REMOVE GIULIANA'S REFERENCES TO HER CONVERSION TO SATANISM, HER FORTHCOMING WEDDING TO SATAN AND HER LOSS OF INNOCENCE.

D. REEL 4   REMOVE THE WHOLE SCENE IN WHICH GIULIANA INTONES PRAYERS TO SATAN AND DRINKS FROM A CHALICE.
REMOVE THE ENTIRE DREAM SEQUENCE.
REDUCE TO A FLASH THE BIRDS' ATTACK ON GIULIANA, REMOVING IN PARTICULAR ALL SHOTS OF HER BLOODSTAINED THROAT, SHOULDERS AND CHEST.
REMOVE ALL SHOTS OF THE "APE" STRUGGLING WITH A GIRL ON THE GROUND.

REEL 9   REDUCE TO A MINIMUM SHOTS OF ALFREDO (IN THE APE COSTUME) CATCHING FIRE AND BURNING.

JULY 1964   PRODUCTION CODE ADMINISTRATION

A copy of a report from the Motion Pictures Association fo America (MPAA) itemizing requested cuts to THE MASQUE OF THE RED DEATH from the British Board of Film Classification (BBFC).

CORMAN/POE

POSTER GALLERY

I RITI, LE MESSE NERE E IL SESSO
DEI SEGUACI DI SATANA
IN CITTA' DEI MOSTRI
CON VINCENT PRICE - DEBRA PAGET - LON CHANEY
Regia: ROGER CORMAN
tratto dai racconti di EDGARD ALLAN POE
TECHNICOLOR - PANAVISION
una produzione A.I.P.

POSTER GALLERY

CORMAN/POE

POSTER GALLERY

AMERICAN INTERNATIONAL PRESENTA
EDGAR ALLAN POE'S
EL CUERVO
VINCENT PRICE
PETER LORRE
BORIS KARLOFF
JACK NICHOLSON
EN PATHECOLOR
DIRIGIDA POR ROGER CORMAN

POSTER GALLERY

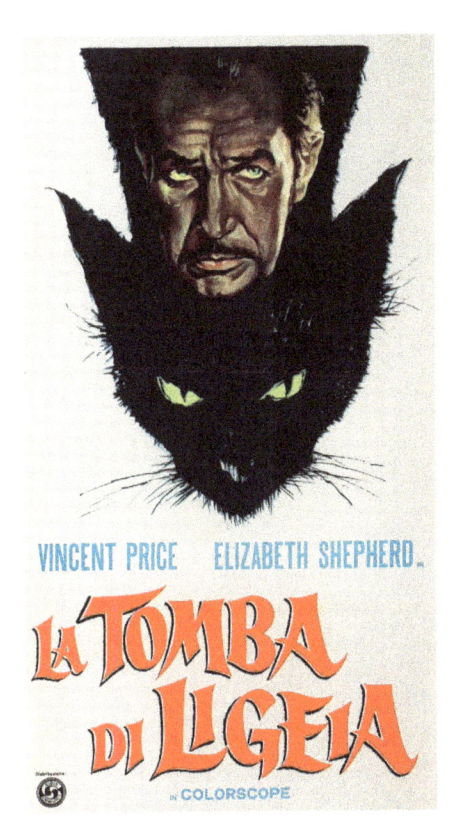

CORMAN/POE

VINCENT PRICE
PETER LORRE
BASIL RATHBONE
DEBRA PAGET
i RACCONTI DEL TERRORE
UN CLASSICO DI EDGAR ALLAN POE
REGIA DI ROGER CORMAN
PANAVISION
UN FILM "AMERICAN INTERNATIONAL"
TECHNICOLOR

EDGAR ALLAN POE'S
ONDSKABENS SLOT
Huset Ushers Fald
I FARVER OG
CINEMASCOPE
med
VINCENT PRICE
MARK DAMON
MYRNA FAHEY
HARRY ELLERBE
PRODUCERET OG ISCENESAT AF
ROGER CORMAN
MANUSKRIPT:
RICHARD MATHESON
Stilling
DS FILM
DYVA & JEPPESENS BOGTRYKKERI A/S KBHVN.

POSTER GALLERY

CORMAN/POE

THE TOMB OF LIGEIA, Dell Comics, 36 pages. On-sale date: February 9th, 1965

POE IN PRINT

THE RAVEN by Eunice Sudak, Lancer Books, mass market paperback, 127 pages. First printing: January 1st, 1963

CORMAN/POE

TALES OF TERROR, Dell Comics, 36 pages. On-sale date: July 26th, 1962
POE'S TALES OF TERROR by Eunice Sudak, Lancer Books, mass market paperback, 126 pages. First printing: January 1st, 1962

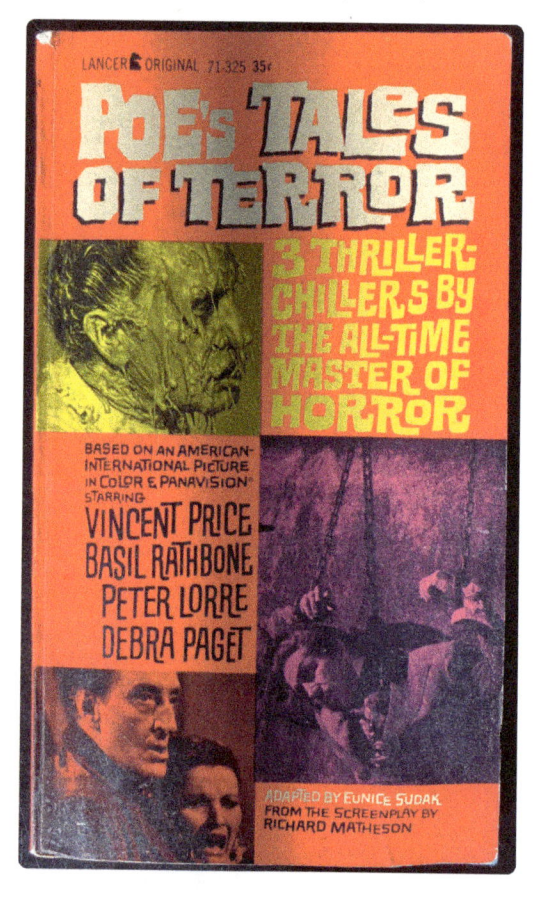

POE IN PRINT

INDEX

A

A BUCKET OF BLOOD 74, 75, 79
Adam, Ronald 112
A MAN FOR ALL SEASONS 103
AMARCORD 3
Anders, Luana 26, 32
Angel, Heather 42
Arkoff, Samuel Z. 12, 15, 20, 21, 26, 42, 54, 70, 84, 90, 112
Asher, Jane 98, 105, 108

B

BAD TIMING 108
Baskin, William 70
Bava, Mario 32, 38, 95
Baxter, Les 12, 19, 22, 26, 31, 37, 51, 54, 70, 84
BEAST FROM HAUNTED CAVE 7
Beaumont, Charles 42, 46, 47, 84, 89, 94, 98, 103, 105, 106, 108, 112, 123
BECKET 103
Bergman, Ingmar 9, 47, 105
BIG GUN, THE 14
BLACK SABBATH 38
BLACK SUNDAY 32, 95
Blackwell, George 98
Brackett, Sarah 98
Bronson, Charlie 21
Brown, Gaye 98
Brown, Scott 54
Bullock, Sandra 34
Buñuel, Luis 47

C

Campbell, R. Wright 98, 103, 106, 112
Campo, Willy 54
Carbone, Anthony 26, 32
Carras, Anthony 12, 26, 54
Chaney Jr., Lon 84, 91, 92, 95
Cobb, Edmund 54
COMEDY OF TERRORS, THE 80
CONQUEROR WORM, THE 95; see also: WITCHFINDER GENERAL
Coodley, Ted 84, 92
Cook Jr., Elisha 84, 95
Coppola, Francis Ford 2, 79, 84, 89
Corey, Jeff 32
Corman, Gene 42
Court, Hazel 42, 47, 51, 70, 81, 98, 104, 109
Cox, Alfred 112
Crosby, Floyd 12, 20, 26, 31, 42, 54, 66, 70, 76, 90, 98, 104, 118
CRY OF THE BANSHEE 108

D

Dalí, Salvador 47
Damon, Mark 12, 18, 19, 22, 23, 29, 38, 39
Dawn, Doreen 98
Deutsch, David 112
DEVIL'S WEDDING NIGHT, THE 38
DeWitt, Alan 54
Dierkes, John 42
Dillon, Brendan 42
Dinga, Pat 12, 26, 54, 70
DON'T LOOK NOW 108
DUNWICH HORROR, THE 95

E

Ellerbe, Harry 12, 84

F

Fahey, Myrna 12, 19
FALL OF THE HOUSE OF USHER, THE 2, 10–23, 30, 31, 34, 35, 37, 38, 47, 50, 51, 60, 63, 80, 105, 109, 122; (*analysis*) 22; (*credits*) 12; (*story*) 14, 15, 16; (*synopsis*) 13
Fellini, Federico 3
FIRE ON THE AMAZON 34
Fisher, Terrence 23
FIVE GUNS WEST 20
Francis, Derek 112
Frankham, David 54, 66

G

Gage, Leona 54
GAS-S-S-S 37
Gilmore, Denis 112
GOLD BUG, THE 120
Gordon, Leo 79, 84, 95
Grant, Arthur 112, 118, 119
Greenlaw, Verina 98
Green, Nigel 98
Green, Pat 112
Griffith, Chuck 75
GUNFIGHTER, THE 14

H

Hackett, John 54
Haller, Daniel 12, 17, 18, 26, 31, 35, 42, 54, 66, 70, 84, 92, 93, 95, 98, 103, 108, 112, 117, 118, 119
Halliday, Clive 42
HAUNTED PALACE, THE 9, 81, 82–95, 120, 122; (*analysis*) 94; (*credits*) 84; (*synopsis*) 85
Hellman, Monte 79
Hessler, Gordon 108

INDEX

Hewlett, Brian 98
HIGH NOON 20
Hill, Jack 79
Hitchcock, Alfred 105

I

I, MOBSTER 92
INTRUDER, THE 89

J

Jameson, Joyce 54, 61, 64
Johnston, Oliver 112
Jolley, I. Stanford 84
Jones, Kenneth V. 112

K

Karloff, Boris 6, 70, 74, 75, 76, 77, 78, 81, 92
Kerr, John 26, 29, 34, 35, 36
Knight, Sandra 79

L

LaCava, Lou 42
Lee, David 98, 108
Lee, Penelope 112
LITTLE SHOP OF HORRORS, THE 7, 75, 78
Lorre, Peter 54, 61, 64, 70, 74, 77, 78, 79
LOST WEEKEND, THE 46
Lovecraft, H.P. 81, 89, 90, 94, 95
Luana, Anders 32, 36
Lucht, Darlene 84

M

MACHINE GUN KELLY 21
Magee, Patrick 98, 106, 109
Maltin, Leonard 7, 9
Martin, Skip 98, 106, 109
MASQUE OF THE RED DEATH, THE 3, 9, 15, 21, 47, 63, 96–109, 117, 118, 122, 126; (analysis) 108; (credits) 98; (synopsis) 99
Matheson, Richard 12, 22, 23, 26, 29, 30, 46, 50, 54, 60, 61, 67, 70, 74, 78, 80, 89, 123

Maxwell, Frank 84
McCartney, Paul 105
Milland, Ray 42, 45, 46, 50, 51, 62, 119
Miller, Dick 42, 47, 51
MONSTER FROM THE OCEAN FLOOR 15
Morris, Barboura 84

N

Napier, Alan 42
Net, Richard 42
Nicholson, Jack 32, 42, 70, 74, 75, 76, 78, 79
Nicholson, James H. 12, 15, 19, 20, 21, 26, 54, 70, 84, 90, 112

P

Paget, Debra 54, 66, 84
Parsons, Milton 84
Peck, Gregory 14
Pierce, Maggie 54
PIT AND THE PENDULUM, THE 9, 24–49, 51, 60, 80, 81, 91, 95, 109, 120, 122; (analysis) 37; (credits) 26; (synopsis) 27; (story) 26
PREMATURE BURIAL, THE 9, 40–51, 62, 119; (analysis) 50; (credits) 42; (synopsis) 43
Price, Vincent 6, 12, 15, 16, 17, 18, 21, 26, 31, 36, 38, 45, 46, 47, 49, 50, 54, 61, 62, 63, 64, 66, 70, 74, 76, 77, 81, 84, 91, 95, 98, 107, 108, 112, 117, 118, 119, 120, 121

R

Rathbone, Basil 54, 63
RAVEN, THE 2, 6, 9, 47, 68–81; (analysis) 80; (credits) 70; (synopsis) 71
Reeves, Michael 95, 108
Roeg, Nicolas 98, 104, 108, 118
Russell, Ray 42, 46, 47, 108

S

Samuels, Ted 112
Saxon, Aaron 70

SECRET INVASION, THE 106
SEVENTH SEAL, THE 105
Shepherd, Elizabeth 112, 120
Shonberg, Bert 18, 34
Sinclair, Ronald 42, 70, 84
Southcott, Colin 112
Steele, Barbara 26, 32, 39, 51
Stein, Ronald 42, 84, 91
Sturgess, Olive 70
Sudak, Eunice 66, 67

T

TABU 20
TALES OF TERROR 9, 52–67, 74, 80; (analysis) 64; (book) 66; (credits) 54; (synopsis) 55
TERROR, THE 79
Thornton, Frank 112
TOMB OF LIGEIA, THE 9, 21, 49, 110–123; (analysis) 122; (credits) 112; (synopsis) 113
Tourner, Jacques 80
Towne, Robert 32, 120, 122
TRIP, THE 37, 121
TWILIGHT ZONE, THE 89, 94

V

VAMPIRE CIRCUS 95
Vernon, Richard 112
VeSota, Bruno 84

W

Wallace, Connie 70
WASP WOMAN, THE 7
Weinrib, Lennie 54
Westbrook, John 112
Weston, David 98
Westwood, Patrick 26
Whitsun-Jones, Paul 98
WILD ANGELS, THE 121
Wilkerson, Guy 84
Willoughby, George 98
WITCHFINDER GENERAL 95, 108

X

X: THE MAN WITH THE X-RAY EYES

A HEADPRESS BOOK

First published by Headpress in 2023, Oxford, United Kingdom
headoffice@headpress.com

CORMAN/POE

INTERVIEWS AND ESSAYS EXPLORING THE MAKING OF ROGER CORMAN'S EDGAR ALLAN POE FILMS, 1960-1964

Text copyright © CHRIS ALEXANDER   This volume copyright © HEADPRESS 2023
Cover design and book layout: MARK CRITCHELL mark.critchell@gmail.com

The Publisher thanks Gareth Wilson.

Special thanks to Jon Davison, Russ Lanier and Julie Corman for all their selfless help and, of course, to the man himself, my friend and forever hero, Roger Corman. Long may he reign.

10 9 8 7 6 5 4 3 2 1

The moral rights of the author have been asserted.
The views expressed in this publication do not necessarily reflect the views of the Publisher.
Images are from the collection of the author and are used for the purpose of historical review.
Grateful acknowledgement is given to the respective owners, suppliers, artists, studios and publishers.
All Rights Reserved. No part of this book may be reproduced, stored in a retrieval system, or transmitted, in any form or by any means, electronic, mechanical, photocopying, recording or otherwise, without prior permission in writing from the publisher.

A CIP catalogue record for this book is available from the British Library

ISBN 978-1-915316-07-3 paperback   ISBN 978-1-915316-08-0 ebook   ISBN NO-ISBN hardback

HEADPRESS. POP AND UNPOP CULTURE

Exclusive NO-ISBN special edition hardbacks and other items of interest are available at **headpress.com**

Milton Keynes UK
Ingram Content Group UK Ltd.
UKHW051931241023
431255UK00006B/54